The US is Dangerous for Women

*Can We Live Safely as Mothers, Wives,
and Business Professionals in a Man's World?*

Teacher, Analyst, Researcher, Author

Joanne Morin Correia

Table of Contents

It is Personal

As a child in the 60s, my best friend Stephen was molested by our guitar teacher on Main Street in Enfield. Ct. When they tried to get me to join them, I ran out of the Music Store and hid in the Catholic church across the street. I feared what I had witnessed, and I did not understand what was happening to my best friend. I told no one and moved to a different school away from Stephen at the end of the school year. We didn't discuss those things back then.

In the mid-1970s, while in high school, Stephen and I worked at the same department store, GFOX, in the mall. He sat next to me, waiting for a ride, and tried to talk to me about what had happened seven years earlier. I couldn't open that door, and I walked away; he committed suicide that night.

It wasn't until my mid-forties, during the radKIDs.org Instructor Training in Sturbridge, Mass., that I finally came to terms with not talking about it when we were training the kids. They need to talk about things when Adults tell them not to, or something bad will happen.

I dedicate this book to Stephen, as he was unaware of the impact of this predictor on him. We need to discuss this to protect our children and others. I wish I had known this that evening and given him more support.

During the late 70s, I went to Bermuda for a College Week of Fun. I rented an apartment with two other women and hung around with a long-time male friend, thinking I would be safer. All week, we danced to a Band called the Bermuda Strollers.

The lead singer asked me on stage to dance several times during the week, and I saw him a few times around the apt. On the final night, he asked me if I would like a tour of the island before I flew home, and if I wanted to see other apartments in case I wanted to return. I said yes.

At his apartment, there were several men, and he pushed me into a bedroom, where there were several knives on the table. He raped me as I pretended to cooperate (I worked for Planned Parenthood, and we were told rapists usually do not murder their victims). Then he took me to the airport, and I boarded my plane to return to Boston. He called me a few years later for a date.

In the 1980s, I traveled the world as a Marketing Manager for Digital Corporation. I had some issues with being followed back to my hotel room and concerns about taxi drivers getting me to my destination. There were no travel-safe guides or mentors available to speak with, which could have helped make it safer. I used my gut, wit, and lessons learned as a tomboy to stay safe.

In the '90s, I was at an IBM event in San Francisco at a "closed" mall with a fantastic band; my male business partner, John, did not want to stay. I told him to leave, and I would taxi back and meet him in the morning.

In less than an hour, I felt like I was going to black out, so I said to the person I was hanging with, I do not feel right, and I headed to the ladies' room. I blacked out before I was able to close the stall door and woke up @30 minutes later; I was date drugged. The ladies helped me get a taxi, and I returned safely to the hotel.

I began my Taekwondo training in my forties and earned my Black Belt at the age of 50. I also trained as an instructor with RAD and radKIDS, teaching over 1,000 students, including my children, friends, and family, through **Common Sense Safety Classes and Rouleau-Holley's Martial Arts.**

Our daughter, Jess, was on a Cruise with us and drugged while she was in a "Safe" Teenage area. She knew enough to get back to us, so several friends on the boat took her to our room.

I watched her go through the stages of being drugged; I called the Doctor on board, and he said, "It was unfortunate, and there was Nothing he could do," but to make sure she did not stop breathing.

On another trip, in broad daylight, Jess was followed, grabbed, and then managed to escape, only to be chased by two men in London, England. She ran into the lobby of a Marriott hotel, and the men turned around and fled. She had the bellman call a taxi for her to return to our hotel, which was several blocks away.

Thankfully, I had trained her to get out of a grab, know where to run, and how to return safely to me, as I had given her taxi money just in case. Jess was also a member of the Cross-Country Team.

At night, sometimes, I replay in my mind the women and children telling their 1,000s of stories of survival when men and women tried to do unspeakable things to them. We taught hundreds of them in our classes as they were filled with children from 3 to 16, foster children, nurses, case workers, teachers, wives, cult escapers, realtors, domestic abuse and rape survivors, and yes, murder witnesses.

Our goal was to make them feel safer despite what had happened. But things changed with the school shootings and other mass shootings. This changes the entire safety scenario because it is unpredictable and aggressive. The authorities often do not know what they do not know or listen to witnesses, and as a result, they fail to act and cannot prevent the violence.

However, there are many good men and women who can make a significant difference in addressing this safety issue. I alone cannot change the world to make it a safer and kinder place.

We can help people learn to rely on their common sense and instincts to be safer while they enjoy their lives, despite what has happened to them.

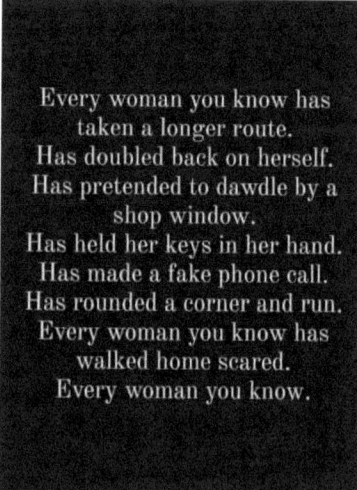

Every woman you know has taken a longer route.
Has doubled back on herself.
Has pretended to dawdle by a shop window.
Has held her keys in her hand.
Has made a fake phone call.
Has rounded a corner and run.
Every woman you know has walked home scared.
Every woman you know.

Thank you for putting up with me.

This journey would not have happened without the love and support of my Husband, Joe, my best friend. Throughout the decades of trying to save the world, I have brought to our "safe" home: horses, dogs, cats, seagulls, and people— women and teenagers just trying to survive.

To our children, Jessica (Jess) and Jonathan (Jon), who trained and taught with me for years. We learned a lot together and helped many people stay safer.

To my manager at Info-Tech, Dave, who supported me by listening to me. And to my friends Shar, Marijane, Sandy, Cat, and others who have helped support me through the multiple versions of this book.

To the martial arts instructors and friends from R+H Taekwondo Do, including Senesi Rouleau, Senesi Buzby, and our radKIDs team of Stephanie and Christine, for encouraging us to instruct children and women in the RAD Systems of Defense and radKIDS.

Combating the Crisis of Violence for Women in the US

End the Stereotypes & Normalization of Violence

All Images Generated by OpenAI's DALL·E [Large language model] (2024 & 2025) unless noted

Living as a woman in America through the 1970s, '80s, and '90s was fraught with danger. Domestic violence was routinely treated as a private family matter, financial dependence on husbands left women with few options for escape, and the law offered minimal protection—marital rape wasn't even recognized as a crime until the 1990s. Over subsequent decades, landmark reforms like the Violence Against Women Act, the criminalization of marital rape, more vigorous restraining-order enforcement, and growing economic opportunities began to chip away at those risks.

Business travel for women in the 1980s and 1990s carried its perils: rampant sexual harassment, discrimination in hotels and taxis, and the absence of cell phones or online support networks to call for help. Today's in-flight safety briefings, 24/7 hotlines, and smartphone apps for lone travelers all grew out of those hard-won lessons.

Yet with President Trump's return to the White House, many of those gains are suddenly under threat. Conservative rollbacks of key VAWA provisions, renewed challenges to reproductive rights, and pandemic-era strains on social services have combined to plunge women's safety into a full-blown national crisis.

Reversals of legal protections and cuts to healthcare and domestic-violence funding now demand an urgent, coordinated response: beefed-up legal enforcement, restored reproductive and mental-health access, workplace training on harassment, and renewed investment in shelters and advocacy networks.

Without swift action, decades of progress risk being undone, and far too many women will again find home and work in dangerous places.

It is a Crisis

Across the United States, women's safety varies widely by issue and geography. Nationally, one in four women will experience severe intimate partner violence, and one in five will face completed or attempted rape during her lifetime. In 2020, roughly 2,000 women were murdered — over half by an intimate partner — and one in six women have been stalked.

Human trafficking disproportionately affects women and girls, with hotspots in major corridors such as California, Texas, and Florida.

Yet these risks are far from uniform: Alaska's rates of domestic and sexual violence can double the national average, while states like New York and Massachusetts report substantially lower homicide and assault figures.

Understanding these patterns by analyzing statistics — both at the national level and in their state-by-state nuances — is crucial to targeting prevention, support, and policy interventions where they are most needed.

Category	National Statistic	State Variation (Examples)
Domestic Violence	1 in 4 women have experienced severe intimate partner violence (CDC)	Alaska: ~50% of women New York: ~25% of women
Sexual Violence	1 in 5 women have experienced completed or attempted rape	Alaska: ~59 incidents per 100,000 New Jersey/Connecticut: ~22–25 incidents per 100,000
Homicide	~2,000 women murdered in 2020; over half by an intimate partner (FBI)	Louisiana: ~2.6 homicides per 100,000 women Massachusetts: ~0.9 homicides per 100,000 women
Stalking	1 in 6 women has been stalked	West Virginia/North Dakota: ~18% of women
Human Trafficking	Women and girls make up most trafficking victims	California: >1,000 cases reported annually High prevalence also in Texas and Florida

Data sources include the CDC's National Intimate Partner and Sexual Violence Survey (NISVS), FBI Uniform Crime Reporting (UCR), and the National Coalition Against Domestic Violence (NCADV).

© 2025 Common Sense Safety Classes

Violence against women is more prevalent in rural areas.

Rural and small-town survivors of intimate partner violence face a constellation of unique obstacles that compound the dangers of abuse. Geographic and social isolation can leave victims cut off from help, while limited law-enforcement presence and sparse support services make it difficult to find safety or legal recourse.

Deeply ingrained cultural expectations and economic dependence further discourage reporting, and ready access to firearms dramatically raises the stakes of any confrontation. Underreporting hides the true scale of the problem, and co-occurring issues like substance abuse and untreated mental health challenges only multiply the risks.

The following sections outline how each of these factors — Isolation, Resource Gaps, Cultural Norms, Economic Dependency, Firearms Access, Underreporting, Substance Abuse, and Mental Health Barriers — intersects to trap too many survivors in silence and danger.

Isolation

In many rural or close-knit communities, survivors face both physical isolation — living miles from essential services or even neighbors — and social isolation, with limited personal networks and a pervasive fear of community retaliation. This dual seclusion means victims often have few safe exit routes and may choose silence over risking ostracism or gossip, trapping them in dangerous situations with little hope of outside relief.

Limited Access to Resources

When law enforcement must cover vast territories with slow response times, and support services like shelters, legal aid, and counseling clinics are scarce or non-existent, survivors can go days or weeks without protection. Without readily available safe houses or affordable legal counsel, it becomes far harder for victims to leave abusive relationships, file restraining orders, or secure the medical and psychological care they need.

Cultural Norms & Attitudes

In communities where conservative gender roles are deeply ingrained and conformity is prized, speaking out against an abusive partner can be seen as defiance of family or tradition. Tight-knit social networks amplify fears of ostracism or shame, pressuring victims to endure harm to preserve communal harmony and their reputation.

Economic Dependency

Limited local employment opportunities and pervasive poverty can leave survivors financially tethered to their abusers, making the cost of relocation or legal action unattainable. The stress of unemployment or underemployment also heightens household tensions, sometimes escalating violence even further.

Firearms Access

High rates of gun ownership in rural and suburban households raise the stakes of domestic disputes, turning heated arguments into potentially lethal encounters. Survivors who know their abuser has ready access to firearms are often too fearful to resist or escape, aware that any attempt to flee could provoke deadly retaliation.

Underreporting of Crimes

In small towns where anonymity is a luxury, survivors may distrust local law enforcement — especially if officers are personally acquainted with the perpetrator — and worry that filing official complaints will make their concerns public knowledge. As a result, official crime statistics can dramatically understate the true prevalence of domestic violence, allowing abusers to act with impunity.

Substance Abuse

Elevated rates of alcohol and drug use in certain regions can fuel cycles of violence, as intoxication lowers inhibitions and increases aggression. Co-occurring addiction issues complicate intervention, since treatment programs may be ill-equipped to address trauma from abuse alongside substance-use disorders.

Mental Health Challenges

With few mental-health professionals serving widespread areas, both victims and perpetrators often go without counseling or psychiatric care. Untreated depression, PTSD, or other illnesses can intensify abusive behaviors or leave survivors without the coping tools they need to break free and rebuild their lives.

These factors combine to create an environment where violence against women can be more frequent and more difficult to escape or address in rural areas compared to urban settings. The complex interplay of geographic, social, economic, and cultural factors makes rural women particularly vulnerable to violence and highlights the need for targeted interventions and resources tailored to these communities.

Patterns of violence are influenced by race, ethnicity, and socioeconomic status.

These patterns are shaped by historical, cultural, social, and institutional factors that affect how violence is perpetrated, reported, and addressed within different communities.

Different racial and ethnic groups experience varying rates of violence against women, which are often influenced by a combination of socio-economic factors, cultural norms, systemic inequality, and access to resources.

Intimate partner violence affects women across every community in the United States. Still, the scale of the problem and the barriers to safety and justice vary dramatically by race and ethnicity.

While overall rates of IPV may appear similar on paper, historical and structural inequities — rooted in racism, colonialism, immigration policy, and cultural stigma — mean that Black, Indigenous, Latina, and Asian and Pacific Islander women often face greater risk, fewer culturally competent resources, and more profound mistrust of legal systems.

Even when survivors do find help, language barriers, underfunded shelters on reservations or in immigrant communities, and fears of deportation or racial profiling can keep them trapped in dangerous situations. Meanwhile, mainstream media coverage tends to spotlight cases involving White women, reinforcing "Missing White Woman Syndrome" and diverting attention and funding away from marginalized survivors.

The following sections examine how prevalence, contributing factors, resource access, and media visibility intersect differently for each group, illuminating the gaps that must be closed to ensure safety and support for all women.

Black Women: Black women face disproportionately high rates of intimate partner violence, with over 40 percent experiencing physical IPV in their lifetimes. This elevated risk is rooted in historical racism and economic disparities that limit financial independence and access to safe housing. Mistrust of law enforcement—fueled by fears of racial bias—and concerns about reinforcing negative stereotypes of Black men further discourage reporting.

As a result, culturally sensitive shelters and legal services are scarce, and community programs are chronically underfunded. While high-profile cases such as Breonna Taylor's death prompt bursts of media coverage and activism, the day-to-day violence endured by Black women remains vastly underreported and under-resourced.

Indigenous Women: Indigenous women endure some of the highest rates of violence in the United States, with more than 84 percent experiencing violence and a murder rate ten times that of non-Indigenous women. This crisis is compounded by centuries of colonial trauma and socio-economic marginalization that concentrate poverty and substance-use issues on many reservations. Jurisdictional confusion between federal and tribal authorities and inadequate law enforcement responses leave survivors with few legal avenues for protection.

On-reserve shelters and support services are minimal, and tribal justice systems are severely underfunded. Although the Missing and Murdered Indigenous Women (MMIW) movement has drawn vital attention to the issue, many individual cases slip through the cracks and receive virtually no sustained media follow-up.

Latina/Hispanic Women: Approximately one-third of Latina and Hispanic women experience physical intimate partner violence, a prevalence shaped by unique barriers. Fear of deportation and insecure immigration status deter many survivors from seeking help, while language differences and cultural stigma around "machismo" and family loyalty further isolate victims. Support services that are bilingual or immigrant-friendly are few, and undocumented survivors often cannot access legal aid.

Locally, community organizations may report on domestic violence within immigrant neighborhoods, but national media attention to Latina survivors of IPV is inconsistent and often overshadowed by broader policy debates.

Asian/Pacific Islander Women: Between 21 percent and 55 percent of Asian and Pacific Islander women report physical or sexual intimate partner violence — yet their experiences are frequently hidden by cultural taboos around family shame and the "model minority" myth. Language barriers and a lack of trust in mainstream social services keep many AANHPI survivors from reaching out.

Programs specifically designed for Asian and Pacific Islander communities are scarce, and outreach to insular or recent-immigrant neighborhoods is limited. Media coverage of AANHPI violence is very low overall, with only a handful of high-visibility cases — such as the tragic deaths of Lauren Cho and Gabby Petito — bringing these systemic issues into the public eye.

White Women: White women experience intimate partner violence at rates comparable to other demographic groups, but they generally face fewer barriers to reporting and accessing help. While social stigma around domestic violence persists, it is less compounded by racial bias, and many survivors maintain greater trust in law enforcement and legal institutions.

A robust network of shelters, hotlines, and legal aid services caters to their needs, and mainstream advocacy campaigns often center on their stories.

Consequently, cases involving White women dominate headlines under the phenomenon known as "Missing White Woman Syndrome," generating more public pressure and resources even as it marginalizes survivors of color.

Patterns Across Groups

- **Underreporting:** Highest among women of color due to distrust, immigration fears, and stigma.
- **Resource Gaps:** Minority women face systemic barriers to culturally competent, accessible services.
- **Media Bias:** White women's cases receive extensive coverage; violence against women of color, predominantly Indigenous and Asian American victims, remains underreported, hampering advocacy and justice efforts.

Patterns of abuse, rape, and violence against women are deeply intertwined with race and ethnicity, influenced by historical, cultural, socio-economic, and institutional factors.

Addressing these patterns requires an intersectional approach that acknowledges the unique barriers and vulnerabilities faced by different groups of women, along with targeted strategies to enhance reporting, access to resources, and legal protections.

There is a lot of evidence of violence and abuse within religious organizations.

The varied forms of violence against women are rooted in religious authority and cultural norms, the mechanisms by which they occur, and their profound personal and social impacts.

However, the nature and extent of this violence can vary significantly depending on the religious context, geographic location, and specific organizational structures.

Category	Mechanisms / Examples	Impact
Sexual Abuse by Clergy	• **Catholic Church:** Documented rape and molestation of nuns and minors by priests • **Other Christian Denominations:** Evangelical and Protestant leaders grooming or coercing women • **Islamic Institutions:** Abuse of female parishioners seeking counseling • **Hindu, Buddhist, Jewish:** Reports of exploitation by religious authorities	• Trauma, PTSD, depression • Erosion of trust in religious institutions • Systemic cover-ups enabling continued abuse
Male Authority & Cultural Silence	• Teachings that justify male dominance and female submission	• Under-reporting of abuse • Prolonged exposure to violence

Category	Mechanisms / Examples	Impact
	• Pressure on women to stay silent about domestic violence to preserve marital unity or family honor • Religious exhortations to "forgive" abusers	• Barriers to seeking help or leaving abusive relationships
Spiritual / Psychological Abuse	• "Spiritual abuse" : Manipulating doctrine to control, shame, or exploit women • Coercive control: Strict dress codes, forced childbearing, and arranged marriages justified by religious law	• Anxiety, depression, loss of autonomy • Internalized shame and self-doubt • Difficulty in recognizing or exiting abuse
Honor-Based Violence	• **Honor Killings:** Murder of women accused of "bringing shame" through behavior or relationships • **Forced Marriages:** Coerced unions to restore family honor	• Femicide and severe physical harm • Life-long psychological trauma • Community-sanctioned impunity

Category	Mechanisms / Examples	Impact
Female Genital Mutilation (FGM)	• Cultural/religious practice of cutting female genitalia to control sexuality • Widely condemned but persists under the guise of tradition	• Chronic pain, infection, and childbirth complications • Severe psychological distress • Violation of bodily autonomy
Institutional Inaction & Reporting Gaps	• Religious bodies disbelieving or shaming victims to protect their reputation • Lack of formal reporting channels; fear of ostracism	• Victims left without recourse • Continued perpetrator impunity • Loss of faith in potential support systems
Violence in Cults & Extremist Groups	• **Totalitarian control:** Forced marriages, sexual slavery, and physical brutality justified by ideology	• Severe physical injury or death • Total loss of personal freedom

Category	Mechanisms / Examples	Impact
	• **Extremist punishments:** Beatings or executions for perceived moral transgressions	• Psychological terror and lifelong trauma
Child Brides & Forced Marriage	• **Religious sanction of under-age marriage** (often as young as 14) with much older spouses • **U.S. legal loopholes:** Parental consent or pregnancy exceptions in states like TX, WV, AR, ID, KY, LA, allowing minors to wed • Immigrant communities upholding traditional early-marriage norms	• Health risks from early pregnancy and childbirth • Interrupted education and economic dependency • Entrapment in lifelong abusive relationships

The #ChurchToo movement, inspired by #MeToo, has spotlighted widespread abuse of women in religious contexts—from clergy sexual assault to domestic violence justified by doctrine, spiritual manipulation, and honor-based violence.

Survivors' testimonies have driven some faith communities to begin implementing explicit reporting channels, victim support services, and disciplinary measures for abusers.

Yet progress remains uneven: many institutions still lack transparent mechanisms or the will to enforce them.

True reform will demand coordinated policy changes, cultural shifts, education for congregations and leaders, and robust support systems to dismantle entrenched power dynamics and safeguard women across all religious traditions.

Women's Participation in Sports remains an ongoing challenge requiring systemic cultural, institutional, and policy shifts.

Safety concerns for women in sports — whether at the professional, college, or high school level — encompass a range of issues, from harassment and abuse to inadequate health and safety measures.

Below, discusses the key safety challenges facing women in sports, spanning abuse, systemic deficiencies, health inequities, cultural biases, and online harassment, and highlight notable examples and their broader impacts.

Women's sports have seen remarkable strides in visibility and professionalism. Yet, female and marginalized athletes continue to confront a web of systemic challenges that jeopardize their safety, well-being, and career trajectories.

From high-profile abuse scandals to everyday shortcomings in policy enforcement, from unequal access to medical care to entrenched cultural biases and relentless online harassment, these issues operate across multiple dimensions of the athletic experience.

There are five core categories — each illustrated by emblematic examples — that highlights the cascading impacts that ripple through individuals, teams, and institutions.

Sexual Harassment & Abuse

High-profile scandals such as the Larry Nassar case in USA Gymnastics — where a trusted team doctor abused hundreds of young women over decades — and the 2021 NWSL revelations of coaches' sexual coercion expose deep failures in safeguarding protocols. When institutions prioritize reputational protection over athlete welfare, survivors are silenced, investigations stall, and predators remain in positions of power.

The psychological damage is profound and long-lasting: victims often struggle with PTSD, loss of trust, and derailed career ambitions. These systemic lapses underscore how even elite organizations can enable abuse when accountability structures are weak or absent.

Safeguards & Reporting Deficits

Across college and high school sports, survivors of assault and harassment frequently encounter opaque complaint processes and face retaliation fears, deterring them from coming forward. Universities have been exposed for mishandling reports to shield their brands, while many secondary school programs lack comprehensive anti-harassment policies or transparent reporting mechanisms. Without clear avenues for safe disclosure and independent review, incidents go unreported, and perpetrators evade consequences. This climate of silence not only re-victimizes athletes but also erodes trust in athletic administrations meant to protect them.

Health & Safety Inequalities

Despite rising awareness of concussion risks, women's soccer players at the collegiate and high-school levels continue to suffer higher rates of head injuries that are often minimized or misdiagnosed. Insufficient investment in gender-specific research, diagnostic protocols, and recovery resources leaves female athletes with slower healing times and heightened risk of long-term cognitive effects. Such disparities extend beyond concussions to broader gaps in training facilities, medical staffing, and performance analytics. When resource allocation favors men's programs, women are left more vulnerable to injury and less supported in rehabilitation, compromising both health and competitive potential.

Cultural & Institutional Barriers

Structural sexism persists in the physical and financial infrastructure of sport, as exemplified by the outcry over the NCAA's superior amenities for men's basketball versus women's teams. Global inequities in media coverage and sponsorship deals further entrench the undervaluation of women's sports, sending a message that female athletes are less marketable or deserving. Transgender and nonbinary competitors face additional exclusion through discriminatory policies and hostile environments. Together, these barriers limit career advancement, foster isolation, and exacerbate mental-health challenges among those who dare to compete outside traditional norms.

Harassment, Threats & Cyberbullying

Even elite champions like Simone Biles and Naomi Osaka have endured virulent online abuse—Osaka in particular receiving threats after prioritizing her mental health at the French Open. Social-media platforms amplify anonymous attacks, turning personal struggles into public spectacles and intensifying anxiety and depression. The pressure to perform under a digital microscope can deter athletes from speaking out or engaging with fans, stripping them of agency and community support. As harassment migrates online, its corrosive effects on mental well-being and public participation demand robust protections and education across all levels of sport.

U.S. military women face numerous safety challenges that impact their service experience and overall well-being.

The following outlines the primary challenges faced by women in military service, organized into eight key categories. For each category, the chart identifies the most pressing issues—ranging from sexual harassment and gender bias to equipment fit and mental health barriers—and illustrates their real-world impacts with concrete examples.

Sexual Harassment & Assault

High rates of unwanted contact and harassment plague many servicewomen, yet deep fears of retaliation or damage to career prospects keep countless incidents from ever being reported. This pervasive silence exacts a heavy toll: survivors are left to contend with PTSD, chronic anxiety, and depression without formal acknowledgment or support.

Gender Discrimination & Bias

Despite formal policies opening combat and leadership roles, women still encounter bias that slows promotions and sidelines them for key assignments. Lingering stereotypes about "fit" and capability undermine unit cohesion and leave female service members excluded from critical career-building opportunities.

Physical & Health Challenges

Standard-issue gear and uniforms engineered for male bodies often fit poorly on women, increasing risk of injury during both training and deployment. Compounding this, access to reproductive and mental-health care is frequently limited — especially in austere or remote postings — leaving women's unique healthcare needs unaddressed.

Mental Health & Support Services

Stigma around seeking psychological help runs especially deep in male-dominated units, where admitting stress or trauma can be seen as weakness. Without confidential, culturally attuned support, many women endure untreated mental-health issues that erode morale and their sense of belonging.

Work-Life Balance & Family Issues

Frequent relocations, deployments, and the lack of reliable childcare place a disproportionate strain on servicewomen — particularly those who are single parents. This family-related stress contributes to higher attrition rates, as many individuals weigh the demands of readiness against the realities of caring for children and maintaining household stability.

Leadership & Representation

Women remain underrepresented in senior ranks and often lack mentors who understand their career challenges. This dearth of role models shrinks the pool of advancement avenues and dampens job satisfaction, reinforcing a cycle that makes it harder for future generations of women to break through.

Safety in Training & Operations

Inappropriate conduct during training exercises and unaddressed vulnerabilities in certain deployment zones deter full participation and reporting. When servicewomen fear both cultural backlash abroad and institutional indifference at home, they're placed at heightened risk and may opt out of critical mission training.

Policy & Cultural Challenges

A predominantly male institutional culture and patchy anti-harassment and discrimination policies slow meaningful reform. Inconsistent enforcement leaves protections unevenly applied, so that even existing rules often fail to safeguard women from bias or abuse.

By framing both the systemic obstacles and their tangible consequences, this chart provides a comprehensive snapshot of the persistent gaps between policy intentions and lived experiences for female service members.

Overall, the data reveal a multifaceted problem: entrenched cultural biases and infrastructural oversights combine to undermine both the safety and career progression of women in uniform. Sexual harassment and assault remain deeply under-reported, while gender discrimination and leadership underrepresentation continue to slow advancement.

Physical challenges — from ill-fitting gear to inadequate healthcare — compound stressors like stigma around mental-health support and work–life conflicts. Together, these factors contribute to higher rates of trauma, attrition, and reduced unit cohesion.

Addressing these issues will require not only policy reform and enhanced enforcement but also a sustained commitment to cultural change, targeted resource allocation for gender-specific needs, and the development of an inclusive leadership pipeline.

The physical, psychological, and institutional challenges impact our women's ability to serve effectively.

2025 Trump-Era Policy Actions

• Rescinded all DOD Diversity, Equity & Inclusion initiatives via executive order
• Forced early retirements and removals of several female generals & admirals from leadership roles

• Eroded career pathways and mentorship networks for women
• Signaled devaluation of gender-diversity efforts, further discouraging retention and promotion of women

These challenges underscore the necessity of ongoing efforts to foster a safer and more inclusive environment for women in the U.S. military, encompassing improved policies, training, support services, and cultural transformation.

Media's Role in the Perpetuation of Violence Against Women

Stereotypes, Normalization of Violence, and Misrepresentation Fuel Gender-based Violence

This is RIDICULOUS !

I mean who needs a "fire to unwind by" when a cold beer with a back massage will do just fine...?

The Good Wife's Guide

From Housekeeping Monthly; May 13, 1955

Have dinner ready. Plan ahead, even the night before, to have a delicious meal ready on time for his return. This is a way of letting him know that you have been thinking about him and are concerned about his needs. Most men are hungry when they get home and the prospect of a good meal is part of the warm welcome needed.

Prepare yourself. Take 15 minutes to rest so you'll be refreshed when he arrives. Touch up your make-up, put a ribbon in your hair and be fresh-looking. He has just been with a lot of work-weary people.

Be a little gay and a little more interesting for him. His boring day may need a lift and one of your duties is to provide it.

Clear away the clutter. Make one last trip through the main part of the house just before your husband arrives. Run a dust cloth over the tables.

During the cooler months of the year you should prepare and light a fire for him to unwind by. Your husband will feel he has reached a haven of rest and order, and it will give you a lift too. After all, catering to his comfort will provide you with immense personal satisfaction.

Minimize all noise. At the time of his arrival, eliminate all noise of the washer, dryer or vacuum. Encourage the children to be quiet.

Be happy to see him. Greet him with a warm smile and show sincerity in your desire to please him.

Listen to him. You may have a dozen important things to tell him, but the moment of his arrival is not the time.

Let him talk first—remember, his topics of conversation are more important than yours.

Don't greet him with complaints and problems. Don't complain if he's late for dinner or even if he stays out all night. Count this as minor compared to what he might have gone through at work.

Make him comfortable. Have him lean back in a comfortable chair or lie him down in the bedroom. Have a cool or warm drink ready for him.

Arrange his pillow and offer to take off his shoes.

Speak in a low, soothing and pleasant voice.

Don't ask him questions about his actions or question his judgment or integrity. Remember, he is the master of the house and as such will always exercise his fairness and truthfulness. You have no right to question him.

A good wife always knows her place. ■

Source: No verifiable copies of *Housekeeping Monthly* have ever published such an article. Its contents closely mirror Helen Andelin's *Fascinating Womanhood* (1963), (en.wikipedia.org)

Over the decades, the media industry has played a significant role in contributing to increased violence against women through various mechanisms.

Early TV sitcoms, such as Leave It to Beaver, Father Knows Best, and The Donna Reed Show, built their humor and "everyday" storylines around very narrow, 1950s-style gender roles.

They:

Cast women almost exclusively as homemakers.

Mothers and wives appear rarely in the workplace; their day is entirely devoted to cooking, cleaning, laundering, child-rearing, and making the home "just so." (Compare, for example, June Cleaver's ever-perfect kitchen in *Leave It to Beaver*.)

Portrayed female happiness as total submission to her husband's needs.

Advice like "have dinner ready, minimize all noise, let him talk first, don't ask him questions about his actions" (as in the 1955 "Good Wife's Guide" image you shared) mirrors the scripts on screen. A woman's most brilliant move was to smile, stay quiet, and defer to her husband's judgment.

Reinforced the male breadwinner/female caretaker power imbalance.

Dad goes off to work with gravitas and authority; Mom exists to support him emotionally, physically, and domestically. By repeatedly portraying this as "normal family life," the shows trained viewers to expect a wife's willing servitude and to view any deviation (a working wife, a vocal wife, or a wife with her agenda) as comic or even improper.

Limited the scope of women's identities.

Female characters rarely have ambitions beyond marriage and motherhood. If they do dare to speak up or pursue outside interests, they're quickly "put back in their place" by well-meaning but firm male figures (husbands, fathers, bosses).

Presented the "ideal wife" as both eternally cheerful and professionally incompetent.

In almost every episode, problems only arise when Mom tries something "new" (a job, a bold opinion, a modern appliance) and must be rescued by Dad's wisdom.

This sends the message that absolute authority and competence lie with men, and that a woman's sphere is the home, if she never questions it.

By normalizing these one-dimensional roles week after week, TV of that era didn't just reflect society's expectations—it actively shaped them, teaching countless viewers that control, authority, and public life belonged to men, while women were happiest—and safest—serving quietly in the domestic realm.

1950s: Perpetuation of Gender Stereotypes

The media predominantly portrays women in traditional domestic roles, reinforcing gender stereotypes of women as homemakers and men as breadwinners.

1960s: Portrayal of Women as Objects

The sexual revolution and changing social norms led to more sexualized portrayals of women in media, beginning the trend of objectification.

1970s: Normalization of Violence

As movies and television shows begin to explore grittier themes, violence against women becomes a common trope, often depicted without consequences.

The 1980s: Hyper-sexualization and Exploitation

Music videos often depicted women in hypersexualized roles, normalizing their objectification and exploitative content with the popularity of slasher films depicting graphic violence.

1990s: Underrepresentation and Stereotypical Representations

Marginalized groups remain underrepresented or portrayed through harmful stereotypes. Emergence of video games featuring graphic violence.

2000s: Influence on Attitudes and Behaviors

Studies show a correlation between the consumption of violent media and aggressive behavior, linking media portrayals to real-life violence. Media increasingly shape cultural norms and values, often portraying violence as acceptable or expected.

The 2010s: Impact of Social Media

Social media leads to increased online harassment, stalking, and abuse with real-life consequences. Amplification of harmful content as platforms amplify misogynistic views and violent imagery, contributing to a culture that condones violence and guns.

2020s: Critical Examination and Reform

Growing awareness and activism led to calls for media reform to promote more accurate, respectful, and diverse representations of women. Media Industry Accountability refers to efforts to hold media creators accountable for depictions that perpetuate violence and stereotypes against women.

2025: Ongoing Efforts:

Continued efforts to address and reduce violence against women through critical examination and reform of media practices.

From perpetuating harmful gender stereotypes to normalizing violence and exploitation, media portrayals often reinforce societal norms that devalue and dehumanize women.

The frequent depiction of women as sexual objects, the glamorization of violence, and the lack of representation of diverse female experiences all contribute to a culture where violence against women is seen as acceptable or inevitable.

As media consumption shapes cultural attitudes and individual behaviors, it becomes crucial to examine critically and reform media practices to promote more accurate, respectful, and diverse representations of women, aiming to reduce the pervasive issue of violence against them.

This table outlines how media mechanisms — from stereotype reinforcement to social-media amplification — shape public perception and can either condone or challenge violence against women.

Category	Mechanisms	Examples & Impact
Perpetuation of Gender Stereotypes	• Portrayal of women as sexual objects • Reinforcement of submissive gender roles	• Women framed as accessories to male leads • "Damsel in distress" tropes normalize power imbalance
Normalization of Violence	• Glamorized or casual depictions of violence against women • Perpetrators shown unpunished	• Domestic-abuse scenes played for drama without real consequences • Viewers are desensitized to the severity of physical or emotional harm

Category	Mechanisms	Examples & Impact
Sexualization & Exploitation	• Over sexualized imagery of women and girls • Depictions of coercive or violent sex	• Music videos that objectify and demean women • Pornographic content that portrays nonconsensual acts as erotic, shaping attitudes toward real-world sexual violence
Misrepresentation & Marginalization	• Under representation of women, especially marginalized groups • Harmful stereotypes (e.g., "angry Black woman," "submissive Asian woman")	• Lack of diverse female leads limits understanding of varied experiences • Stereotypes reinforce myths (e.g., that some groups are less credible as victims)
Influence on Attitudes & Behaviors	• Correlation between media violence consumption and real-world aggression	• Studies link violent films/games to increased acceptance of aggression • Persistent "boys will be boys"

Category	Mechanisms	Examples & Impact
	• Repeated depictions shape cultural norms	framing makes disrespectful behavior more socially acceptable
Impact of Social Media	• Harassment, stalking, and doxxing of women online • Rapid spread of misogynistic or violent imagery	• Viral shaming campaigns discourage reporting of abuse • Algorithms amplify harmful content, reinforcing echo chambers that condone violence
Trump-Era Media Amplification	• High-profile misogynistic remarks normalized by relentless coverage • Polarizing debate that both spreads and critiques abusive rhetoric	• Some audiences grew numb to derogatory comments; others mobilized under #MeToo • Media focus on Trump's behavior spurred policy discussions but also risked "overexposure fatigue."

Industry Examples	• Television & Film • Music Videos • Advertising • Video Games	• Soap operas gloss over spousal abuse without repercussion • Ads use nudity to sell unrelated products • Games depict graphic violence without moral framing

Sources: https://www.domesticviolenceinfo.ca/resources

The media industry's role in contributing to violence against women spans several decades through the perpetuation of harmful gender stereotypes, normalization of violence, hyper-sexualization, misrepresentation, and influence on societal attitudes. Efforts to address these issues must include critical examination and reform of media practices, alongside promoting respectful and diverse representations of women.

Trump's Impact on Media Coverage

Misogynist Tendencies Harm Safety and Perception of Women

Over the past decade, media coverage of Donald Trump's controversial views on women and his bullying tendencies has significantly influenced the safety and perception of women in the U.S.

This amplification of high-profile behavior — Trump's pronouncements alongside the loud public debates around them — has sometimes normalized misogyny and emboldened aggressive conduct. Yet at the same time, it has increased awareness of gender-based violence and fueled grassroots movements like #MeToo, creating new spaces for survivors to speak out and for allies to push for change.

When Supreme Court nominee Brett Kavanaugh's 2018 confirmation hearings erupted around multiple allegations of sexual assault — most prominently those brought forward by Dr. Christine Blasey Ford — the media played much the same double-edged role. Wall-to-wall coverage of Ford's testimony and Kavanaugh's emotional rebuttals shone a harsh spotlight on how seriously the nation takes (or dismisses) accusations against powerful men.

On one hand, some audiences bristled at what they saw as a media-driven "trial by public opinion," reinforcing a siege mentality that women's claims are just another partisan weapon. On the other hand, the hearings forced an unflinching national conversation about consent, due process, and the systemic barriers survivors face, driving both policy proposals and cultural shifts toward believing and supporting women.

The Jeffrey Epstein saga added yet another layer to this complex media dynamic. Coverage of Epstein's arrest on federal sex-trafficking charges in 2019, the explosive revelations about his vast network of underage victims, and the controversies surrounding his death in custody thrust the issue of elite-enabled abuse into the headlines.

Media outlets wrestled with questions about who enabled Epstein's crimes — and why so many influential figures remained above scrutiny. While some commentary veered into sensationalism or conspiracy mongering, the relentless reporting also shone a bright light on the horrors of sex trafficking, the failures of our justice system, and the urgent need for accountability at every level.

Together, the narratives around Trump, Kavanaugh, and Epstein have underscored that public visibility of alleged misconduct can both retraumatize survivors and catalyze reform. By repeatedly placing women's safety and men's accountability front and center, these storylines have contributed to an environment where women's experiences are more widely acknowledged, even as real progress remains uneven and contested.

Donald Trump has faced multiple allegations and been convicted of sexual misconduct over the years, with accusations ranging from sexual harassment to assault.

Individual	Accusations	Legal Action / Payment	Outcome / Consequences
E. Jean Carroll	Allegedly, Trump sexually assaulted her in a department store in the 1990s.	Filed a defamation suit after Trump denied the claim.	Found liable (2023); Trump ordered to pay $5 million in damages.
Stormy Daniels	Claimed an affair with Trump in 2006 and later threats to silence her.	Michael Cohen paid her $130,000 in hush money (2016) at Trump's direction.	Triggered campaign-finance investigations; Cohen pleaded guilty (2018).
Karen McDougal	Allegedly had a 10-month affair with Trump in 2006–2007.	Sold her story to AMI for $150,000 under a "catch-and-kill" agreement (2016).	AMI's handling scrutinized in campaign-finance probes; no direct lawsuit by McDougal.
Other Allegations	Over 20 women have accused Trump of groping, unwanted kissing, harassment, or assault across decades.	Most did not result in legal filings; Trump has uniformly denied wrongdoing and called claims politically motivated.	No further civil or criminal judgments beyond Carroll; allegations continue to shape public debate.

Some cases have concluded, while others remain open to future litigation. The legal ramifications have varied, with some cases resulting in monetary settlements and others leading to ongoing investigations or civil suits.

The high-profile nature of these cases involving Donald Trump — and the public discourse around them — has had broader social impacts, contributing to a complex landscape regarding violence toward women. These cases, along with others, influence attitudes and behaviors in society.

Theme	Description	Impact
Normalization & Perception of Misconduct	Public figures accused of sexual misconduct often face little accountability, creating a sense that powerful men are "above the law."	Survivors may feel their allegations won't be taken seriously and are discouraged from reporting abuse.
Increased Awareness & Divided Responses	High-profile cases (e.g., Trump) fueled #MeToo and public discussion, but also polarizing debate, with some doubting allegations as politically motivated.	While some rally behind survivors, partisan divides hinder a universally supportive environment, complicating efforts to validate and aid victims.

Theme	Description	Impact
Reporting & Justice for Survivors	More women come forward after high-visibility cases, yet systemic barriers persist when influential accused individuals face minimal consequences.	Feelings of helplessness and resignation among survivors reinforce the belief that reporting will not lead to justice or support.
Backlash & Misogynistic Rhetoric	Social-media backlash often involves shaming or blaming survivors, with a resurgence of derogatory language targeting accusers.	Creates a toxic environment that silences victims and may embolden others to adopt or express harmful attitudes toward women.
Legal & Policy Impacts	Public outcry has driven the development of stronger anti-harassment policies and reporting mechanisms in workplaces and institutions.	Policy reforms exist, but they often lack effective systemic enforcement, which limits their ability to protect survivors and change organizational culture.
Potential Influence on Public Behavior	When influential individuals escape consequences, their behavior can tacitly signal social acceptance of dismissive or disrespectful attitudes toward women.	May normalize nonviolent but harmful misconduct, making disrespectful or demeaning behavior toward women more socially acceptable, even if not directly increasing violence.

After The 2024 Election

The Lasting Impact of Gender Dynamics in the Harris–Trump Rematch

The 2024 rematch between Vice President Kamala Harris and former President Donald Trump once again thrust America's fraught gender dynamics into the national spotlight. Trump's prior tenure had normalized a tough-talking, often sexist political style, while Harris's groundbreaking candidacy embodied the promise of a new era for women's leadership.

Yet, in a result that stunned many, Harris fell short, and Trump reclaimed the White House. This chapter examines how decades-long patterns of media portrayal, societal attitudes, and political polarization combined to shape both the campaign and its outcome, and what this means for the future of women's rights and safety in the United States.

Normalization of Misogyny in Political Discourse

Theme	Description	Impact
Erosion of Respect	Post-2020 surveys showed increased tolerance for sexist language, especially among younger men, mirroring Trump's derogatory remarks.	Sexist remarks become "background noise," lowering barriers to everyday misogyny.

Theme	Description	Impact
Media Reinforcement	Pundits repeatedly replayed salacious soundbites as "locker-room talk," framing them as harmless political banter.	Further dulled public sensitivity and normalized demeaning commentary toward women.

Amplified #MeToo Momentum & Its Limits

Element	Positive Outcomes	Limitations
Cultural Shift	More survivors felt empowered; several states passed stricter harassment penalties and extended statutes of limitation.	Deep partisan divide: Many conservatives dismissed #MeToo as a partisan attack.
Political Leverage	Harris' campaign pledged swift accountability and stronger protections for survivors, capitalizing on the momentum of the #MeToo movement.	Limited sway over undecided or skeptical male voters in key swing states.

Policy Battles & Political Gridlock

Arena	Advancements (State Level)	Stalemate (Federal Level)
Workplace Protections	New anti-harassment laws in several states	Comprehensive federal bills were blocked by Republican-led chambers, citing fiscal and ideological concerns.
Violence Prevention	Expanded funding for women's shelters in multiple jurisdictions	VAWA reauthorization and related measures stalled in Congress

Implications for Women's Safety

Signal	Observation
Emboldened Bullying	Domestic-violence hotlines saw a slight spike in calls during and after Trump rallies.
Heightened Vigilance	Advocacy groups reported record numbers of volunteer sign-ups and donations for women's safety organizations.

The Missing Teachable Moment: Masculinity & Accountability

Expectation	Reality
Nationwide Dialogue	Scholars hoped Trump's controversies would spark discussion on healthy masculinity.
Outcome	Many young men still idolize aggressive "strength"; widespread cynicism remains over the lack of consequences.

Why Harris Lost

Ignoring the evidence of election manipulation, which is forthcoming, several other intertwined factors explain Harris's narrow defeat:

Factor	Description
Entrenched Partisan Loyalties	Trump retained near-the ceiling Republican support by portraying opponents as elitist and out of touch.
Gender Bias in Swing Voters	Post-election polls showed ~20% of undecided voters doubted a woman's leadership ability during a crisis.

Factor	Description
Media Fatigue & Overexposure	Constant scandal coverage bred voter exhaustion, prompting some to opt for the perceived stability of Trump over continued controversy.
Economic Anxiety & Single-Issue Voting	Inflation and security concerns led many to prioritize Trump's economic and border-security promises over gender-equality initiatives like harassment laws.

The 2024 Harris–Trump rematch laid bare the persistent power of gendered narratives in American politics. Trump's brand of normalized misogyny, coupled with deep polarization and unyielding partisan identities, proved a formidable barrier to change. Yet the campaign also catalyzed unprecedented activism around women's rights, legal accountability, and the struggle for respectful leadership. Harris's loss underscores the distance still to travel: even as women's voices grow louder, transforming cultural attitudes and holding leaders accountable remains urgent.

Violence Against Women Act (VAWA) and Title 9

Addressing Funding, Legal Gaps, Accessibility, Cultural Barriers, and Evolving Threats for Survivors

LEGAL AND DUE PROCESS

The Violence Against Women Act (VAWA) is a landmark piece of legislation in the United States aimed at addressing and reducing domestic violence, sexual assault, and other forms of violence against women. Its history is marked by significant legislative milestones, bipartisan support, and continued evolution to address emerging issues.

Violence Against Women Act (VAWA) – History & Key Milestones

Period	Action	Details
1990s	Introduction & Initial Passage	• 1990: Introduced by Sen. Joe Biden in response to rising awareness of domestic violence/sexual assault • 1994: Enacted as part of the Violent Crime Control Act; created DOJ's Office on Violence Against Women; funded shelters, hotlines, & federal penalties
2000	First Reauthorization	Expanded protections for battered immigrants; added funding for rape-prevention education; created teen dating-violence programs.

2005	Second Reauthorization	Added initiatives for Native American women; bolstered services for sexual-assault victims; enhanced anti-trafficking measures; strengthened legal protections.
2013	Third Reauthorization	After a contentious fight, extended coverage to LGBTQ+ survivors, undocumented immigrants, and Native Americans; addressed campus sexual violence; and empowered tribal courts to prosecute non-Native offenders for on-reservation abuse.
2017–2021	Debate & Lapse	Disputes over: gun-control ("boyfriend loophole"), LGBTQ+ protections, tribal-court jurisdiction, and funding levels. Partisan gridlock led to expiration in 2018 and

		gaps in some services; House passed a new bill in 2021.
2022	**Fourth Reauthorization**	Signed into law in March 2022 as part of the omnibus spending bill, the bill improved access to services for survivors, boosted culturally specific programs, and strengthened prevention efforts.
2025	Gender-equity protections under Title IX have undergone a legal reversal even as investigatory efforts ramp up.	DODJ's freeze on VAWA-related grants threatens critical services for survivors of gender-based violence. The net effect is a patchwork of advances and setbacks for women's programs during the first 100 days of the current administration.

In the first 100 days of 2025, key federal programs affecting women underwent significant changes.

Title IX enforcement regressed when a court overturned the Biden administration's 2024 regulations, reverting to the stricter 2020 rules, while simultaneously launching a new DOJ/ED Special Investigations Team to target systemic campus civil rights abuses.

The Violence Against Women Act's grant programs were thrown into limbo by an unexpected OVW funding freeze, imperiling shelters and legal-advocacy nonprofits.

And, after threats of termination, the Women's Health Initiative study received a last-minute funding reprieve on April 28, although its long-term stability remains in question.

Program	Action	Date	Implications
Title IX Enforcement	Vacatur of Biden-era 2024 Final Rule; reversion to Trump regulations	Jan 9, 2025	Schools now enforce the narrower 2020 Title IX standards, potentially reducing protections for survivors of sexual harassment and assault.
	Launch of joint Title IX Special Investigations Team	Early Apr 2025	DOE & DOJ to pursue systemic civil-rights violations in education, signaling tougher, targeted enforcement under the reverted rule.

Program	Action	Date	Implications
VAWA Grants & OVW Funding	Abrupt funding freeze; removal of all open grant solicitations from OVW site	Feb 2025	Nonprofits face uncertainty; emergency shelters and legal-advocacy services risk scaling back or closure without clarity on future awards.
Women's Health Initiative (WHI) Study	Reversal of planned HHS termination; funding secured	Apr 28, 2025	WHI study — tracking cancer risk, hormone therapy, aging in 160,000+ postmenopausal women — continues, though long-term researcher support remains uncertain.

The US is a Rape Culture

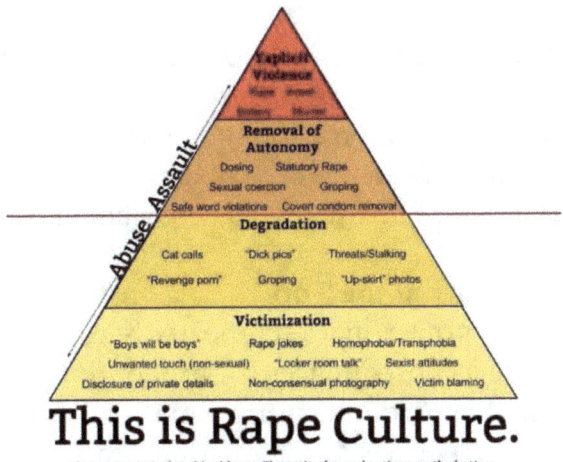

As Kamala Harris squared off against Donald Trump, it wasn't just a rematch of personalities — it was a stark reminder that, in America today, women are navigating a landscape rife with a rape culture and entrenched misogyny that politics alone has failed to tame.

How the U.S. has become dangerously unsafe for women:

- **Normalization of Sexual Violence**
  From locker rooms to cable news, derogatory remarks and demeaning jokes about women have seeped into everyday conversation. This constant drip of disrespect erodes our collective understanding of consent and fuels an environment where sexual harassment and assault are dismissed as "boys being boys."

- **Impunity at the Top**
  When powerful men repeatedly escape serious consequences for misconduct — whether through courtroom victories, overturned verdicts, or faded headlines-it sends a message far beyond the courthouse: that women's bodies and voices are expendable when stacked against wealth or status.

- **Politicization over Protection**
  Rather than view violence against women as a human-rights crisis, lawmakers too often treat reform as a pawn in partisan battles. Critical protections — like explicit, survivor-centered Title IX processes or full funding for the Violence Against Women Act — stall not because they lack merit, but because they conflict with political agendas.

Cultural Forces Deepening the Danger

- **Toxic Masculinity as Idolization**
  Aggression, dominance, and emotional
  unavailability are still widely celebrated as
  "strength." With few alternative role models
  amplified in our schools, media, and sports, many
  young men equate manhood with power over
  women rather than with respect or empathy.

- **Rape Myths and Victim Blaming**
Myths— "She was asking for it," "Women lie about assault"—endure in headlines and social media comments. Each time a victim is doubted or shamed, it reinforces the false narrative that women are responsible for the violence inflicted upon them.

- **Cynicism Toward Justice**
Public frustration grows when disparate standards apply: a viral scandal for some, but a shrug for others. As faith in courts and legislatures erodes, fewer survivors come forward, and fewer bystanders speak up, deepening the culture of silence.

Why Politics Cannot Fix Rape Culture Alone

- **Superficial Reforms**
  Mandates and task forces are launched with fanfare, yet meaningful change — retraining for law enforcement, comprehensive sex ed in schools, survivor-led support services — remains underfunded or unfunded.

- **Election-Year Posturing**
  Candidates queue up for photo opportunities with activists or tout "women's safety" platforms, but once votes are counted, many of these measures disappear from the agenda. The cycle of outrage then lulls, leaving women more vulnerable, not less.

- **Lack of Cross-Partisan Commitment**
  Until violence against women unites rather than divides, every proposed improvement risks becoming another casualty of gridlock — trapped in the Land of Endless Hearings and No Votes.

Turning the Tide: Beyond Campaign Rhetoric

- **Center Survivors' Voices**
  True reform begins when survivors, not pollsters or pundits, set the agenda. That means listening without skepticism, funding

community-based support, and enshrining their recommendations in law.

- **Reimagine Masculinity**
  From classroom curricula to corporate leadership programs, we need a national campaign that elevates empathy, accountability, and partnership as the objective markers of strength.

- **Sustain Legislative Will**
  Safe schools, fully staffed crisis centers, and trauma-informed policing require multi-year funding commitments, with automatic renewals unless explicitly sunset. In other words, prioritize women's safety as a nonpartisan infrastructure, not an annual budget fight.

US vs Other Industrialized Nations

Reduce Violence, Strengthen Legal Practices, and Promote Gender Equality

Women's safety in the United States is a complex and nuanced issue. Various factors contribute to the perception and reality of danger, including crime rates, legal protections, cultural attitudes, and social services.

Factors Affecting Women's Safety in the U.S.

- **Crime Rates:** The U.S. has some of the highest rates of violent crime compared to many other industrialized nations, including incidents of domestic violence and sexual assault. The prevalence of gun violence also impacts overall safety.

- **Legal Protections and Resources:** The U.S. has robust legal protections for women, including laws against domestic violence, sexual assault, and workplace harassment. While some organizations and shelters provide support to women in danger, they are overloaded and have wait times.

- **Cultural and Social Factors:** Cultural attitudes towards women vary widely across regions and communities. Social issues, including poverty, limited access to healthcare, and educational disparities, can also impact women's safety and well-being.

- **A decade of interplay of GOP policies:** A series of GOP-driven decisions — most prominently the 2022 reversal of Roe v. Wade and pandemic-era policy responses — have compounded risks to women's safety and eroded hard-won gains in gender equality.

Comparison to Other Industrialized Nations

Category	U.S.	Other Industrialized Nations
Violent Crime Rates	Relatively high	Generally lower (e.g., Sweden, Germany, Netherlands)
Social Welfare Supports	Less comprehensive	More robust (especially in Nordic countries)
Gun Violence	Very high (highest civilian gun ownership)	Low (strict gun laws; minimal gun-related violence)
Cultural Attitudes	Weak emphasis on gender equality	Strong emphasis on women's rights and non-tolerance of violence

While the U.S. has many resources and legal protections for women, it has higher rates of violent crime and gun violence, along with varying cultural attitudes, which can make it a more dangerous place for women compared to many other industrialized nations. However, the situation can vary significantly depending on specific locations and communities within the U.S.

Statistical Comparisons

According to the Global Peace Index and other safety rankings, the U.S. ranks lower in overall safety compared to many European and industrialized countries. Reports such as the World Economic Forum's Global Gender Gap Index can provide insights into how different countries rank.

Metric	United States	European Union
Homicide Rate by Firearms (Women)	~1.8 per 100,000 women	~0.2 – 0.4 per 100,000 women
Firearm-Related Death Rate (Overall, Including Suicides)	~3.6 per 100,000 women	< 0.5 per 100,000 women
Intimate Partner Homicides Involving Firearms	~50 % of cases	< 20 % of cases

Key Points:

- **Comparison:** Women in the U.S. are approximately 4 to 9 times more likely to die from firearm-related violence compared to women in the EU.
- **Higher Risk:** The elevated rates in the U.S. are attributed mainly to the greater availability of firearms, less restrictive gun control laws, and a higher prevalence of gun violence.

Home Remains the Most Dangerous Place for US Women

Four Decades of Domestic Violence, Financial Dependency, and Evolving Legal Protections

For the past four decades, and continuing today, the home has been the most dangerous place for many women in the United States. Despite significant strides in legal protections and societal awareness, domestic violence remains a pervasive threat fueled by financial dependency, entrenched societal norms, and inconsistent legal enforcement.

Abusers exploit the privacy and isolation of the home to exert control, leaving victims vulnerable to severe physical, psychological, and emotional harm. This article explores the reasons behind this enduring threat, examining historical and contemporary challenges and highlighting the ongoing need for robust interventions and support systems.

Domestic Violence Prevalence and Impact

- **High Incidence:** Domestic violence remains a pervasive issue, with intimate partner violence affecting millions of women annually. The National Coalition Against Domestic Violence reports that one in four women experiences severe intimate partner violence in their lifetime.

- **Severity:** Domestic violence can escalate to severe physical abuse, sexual assault, psychological trauma, and even homicide. The Centers for Disease Control and Prevention (CDC) indicate that over half of female homicide victims are killed by intimate partners.

Psychological and Emotional Abuse

- **Control and Manipulation:** Abusers often exert psychological control over their victims, using tactics like isolation, intimidation, and emotional manipulation to maintain dominance.
- **Impact on Mental Health:** Continuous exposure to such abuse can lead to long-term mental health issues, including depression, anxiety, and post-traumatic stress disorder (PTSD).

Financial Dependency and Economic Barriers

- **Lack of Financial Independence**: Many women, especially those in traditional housewife roles, may lack their own income or financial resources, making it difficult to leave abusive relationships.

- **Economic Abuse:** Abusers often control household finances, restricting access to money and financial information, further trapping victims in dangerous situations.

Societal Attitudes and Norms

- **Historical and Cultural Context:** Normalization of Abuse: Historically, domestic violence was often seen as a private matter, with societal norms discouraging outside intervention. This normalization has perpetuated a culture of silence and tolerance around domestic abuse.
- **Victim Blaming**: Victims of domestic violence frequently face societal stigma and victim-blaming, discouraging them from seeking help or speaking out about their experiences.

Legal Protection and Law Enforcement

- **Variable Enforcement**: Although significant legal progress has been made, the enforcement of domestic violence laws varies widely by jurisdiction. Inconsistent responses from law enforcement and the judicial system can leave victims vulnerable.

- **Restraining Order:** Although restraining orders are available, their effectiveness depends on prompt and strict enforcement. Violations of restraining orders are not always adequately addressed, putting victims at continued risk of abuse and even homicide.

Seclusion and Control
- **Isolation Tactics**: Abusers often isolate their victims from friends, family, and support networks, making it harder for them to seek help or escape.
- Privacy of the Home: The private nature of the home can make it difficult for others to detect or intervene in cases of domestic violence. Abusers exploit this privacy to control and harm their victims without outside interference.

Today's Challenges and Improvements

- **Technology and Abuse**: Modern technology has introduced new forms of abuse, such as cyberstalking and digital surveillance, which abusers can use to exert control over their victims.
- **Pandemic Impact**: The COVID-19 pandemic exacerbated domestic violence, as lockdowns and social distancing measures increased isolation and limited access to support services.

Legal and Social Progress

- **Legislative Advances**: Laws like the Violence Against Women Act (VAWA) have significantly improved legal protections and resources for domestic violence victims.
- **Support Services**: Increased funding and availability of shelters, hotlines, and advocacy programs provide critical support for women in dangerous home environments.

The home has historically been, and continues to be, a dangerous place for many women in the United States due to the pervasive nature of domestic violence, financial dependency, societal attitudes, and challenges in legal enforcement. While significant progress has been made regarding legal protections and support services, continued efforts are necessary to address these issues and ensure the safety and well-being of women in their own homes.

Today, housewives face numerous financial challenges that can impact their economic security and independence.

Financial Dependency:
- **Single Income Reliance**: Many housewives rely on their spouse's income, which can create financial vulnerability if the spouse loses their job, falls ill, or the couple divorces.

- **Limited Personal Income**: Without a personal income, housewives often have limited access to financial resources, making it challenging for them to contribute to household expenses or save.

Retirement and Savings:
- **Insufficient Retirement Savings**: Housewives who do not work outside the home may not have personal retirement savings or access to employer-sponsored retirement plans, leading to financial insecurity in old age.
- **Dependence on Spouse's Pension:** They often rely on their spouse's pension or retirement accounts, which may not be sufficient or guaranteed in the event of divorce or the spouse's death.

Access to Credit
- **Building Credit History:** With personal income or credit accounts, housewives may be able to build a strong credit history, which can impact their ability to secure loans or mortgages independently.
- **Joint Accounts:** Relying on joint accounts can limit their financial autonomy and complicate financial situations during separation or divorce.

Economic Opportunities

- **Employment Gap**: Housewives who return to the workforce after years of staying at home often face challenges due to employment gaps, which can affect their employability and salary potential.
- **Skill Development:** Keeping skills up-to-date or acquiring new ones can be made easy with the time and financial resources to invest in education or training.

Healthcare and Insurance

- **Dependent Coverage:** Housewives often rely on their spouse's employer-provided health insurance. Changes in the spouse's employment status can lead to loss of coverage and increased healthcare costs.
- **Personal Healthcare Plans:** Obtaining personal health insurance can be costly and complicated without an employer's group plan.

Legal and Financial Planning

- **Estate Planning:** Lack of involvement in financial planning can lead to inadequate estate planning, leaving housewives financially insecure in case of their spouse's death.

- **Knowledge of Finances:** Limited expertise and involvement in family finances can make it difficult to manage finances independently after divorce or widowhood.

Childcare and Education Costs
- **Rising Costs:** The increasing costs of childcare and education can strain the household budget, mainly when relying on a single income.
- **Savings for Children:** Without personal income, balancing savings for children's education and other needs with household expenses can be challenging.

Inflation and Cost of Living
- **Rising Costs:** The increasing cost of living, including housing, utilities, and groceries, can put additional financial pressure on single-income households.
- **Budgeting**: Effective budgeting becomes crucial but challenging, especially with unpredictable expenses and rising prices.

Access to Financial Education and Resources
- **Lack of Financial Literacy:** Limited access to financial education can hinder housewives' ability to manage finances effectively and make informed financial decisions.

- Resource Availability: Without awareness or access, finding and utilizing resources such as financial advisors or community support programs can be difficult.

Strategies to Mitigate Financial Challenges

Financial Planning: Engage in comprehensive financial planning with your spouse, including budgeting, savings, and investment strategies that align with your goals.

- **Building Credit:** Establish and maintain personal credit accounts to build a strong credit history.
- **Retirement Savings:** Contribute to retirement savings through individual retirement accounts (IRAs) or spousal IRAs.
- **Continuing Education:** Pursue education and skill development opportunities to enhance employability and potential earnings.
- **Healthcare Planning:** Explore healthcare options and ensure coverage if the spouse's employment status changes.
- **Legal Protections: Stay** informed about legal rights and protections, including prenuptial agreements and estate planning.
- **Financial Independence:** Develop independence by exploring part-time work, freelance opportunities, or home-based businesses.

Modern-day housewives face various financial challenges, from dependency on a single income to difficulties in building personal credit and securing retirement savings. Addressing these challenges requires proactive financial planning, continuous education, and access to resources and support systems that promote economic independence and security.

The more chances you give someone the less respect they'll start to have for you. They will begin to ignore the standards that you've set because they'll know another chance will always be given. They're not afraid to lose you because they know no matter what you won't walk away. They get comfortable with depending on your forgiveness. Never let a person get comfortable disrespecting you.

High-Risk Occupations

Understanding the Most Violent Jobs and Strategies for Enhancing Safety and Support

Women face significant risks in specific jobs and environments, leading to heightened concerns about safety and violence. Professions such as healthcare, education, social work, law enforcement, and retail are dangerous due to the high potential for physical assaults and volatile situations.

Similarly, certain urban areas with high crime rates, remote and isolated work sites, public transportation systems, and shelters for the homeless pose additional threats. Understanding these dangers is crucial for implementing effective safety measures and ensuring the protection of women in these high-risk settings.

Most Violent Jobs and Places for Women

- **Healthcare Workers:** Nurses and caregivers often face workplace violence, including physical assaults by patients. The high-stress environment and close contact with patients can increase the risk of violent incidents. Home healthcare workers are particularly vulnerable because they work in clients' homes, often alone, and may encounter dangerous situations without immediate support.

- **Education Professionals**: Teachers and educational assistants have reported increased incidents of violence, including physical attacks by students or even parents. This trend is alarming in the US, where recent incidents have underscored the dangers associated with this field.

- **Social Workers**: Public Service roles frequently deal with high-risk populations and volatile situations, such as domestic violence cases and mental health crises. These interactions can lead to dangerous confrontations, making this a high-risk profession for women.

- **Law Enforcement and Security Personnel**: Police officers and security guards face inherent danger, including violent confrontations with criminals. Female officers and guards are particularly at risk due to the physical nature of the job and potential targeting by offenders.

- **Retail and Hospitality Workers**: Retail workers, especially those working late shifts, are at risk of robberies and assaults. Similarly, hospitality workers such as hotel staff and bartenders can encounter aggressive behavior from patrons, often exacerbated by alcohol consumption.

Dangerous Places for Women

- **Urban Areas with High Crime Rates:** Cities like *Detroit, Baltimore, and St. Louis in the US have high violent crime rates, making them particularly dangerous for women.

- **Remote and Isolated Areas**: Remote work sites, such as those in the logging, mining, and fishing industries, pose significant risks due to isolation and limited access to emergency services. Women working in these environments are particularly vulnerable to assaults and accidents.

- **Public Transportation**: Women using public transportation late at night or in poorly lit areas are at risk of harassment and assault. Ensuring safety in these environments remains a critical concern in both countries.

- **Housing and Homeless Shelters**: Shelters and transitional housing facilities can be dangerous due to the high concentration of individuals with complex needs, including those with histories of violence. Women in these settings may face threats from other residents or external visitors.

The most dangerous and violent jobs and places for women in the US span various sectors and locations, from healthcare and education to urban centers and remote worksites. Addressing these risks requires comprehensive strategies, including improved workplace safety measures, better support systems, and robust legal protections to ensure women's safety across all environments.

One of the areas in which I have conducted many workshops is real estate, schools, and hospitals, as these are high-risk professions for women. Real estate work poses significant hazards for women due to several inherent risks associated with the job. Female real estate agents often work alone, meeting clients at various properties, leaving them vulnerable to attacks.

My friend Lee has been attacked multiple times, with two of the assailants being sentenced to jail time. Put into jail. She would not be here with us on earth without carrying personal safety items.

Here are some key factors and examples highlighting the dangers faced by women in this profession:

- **Working Alone:** Female real estate agents often work alone, making them vulnerable to attackers who can track their whereabouts through social media and scheduled appointments. The nature of the job, which involves showing properties to strangers, increases the risk of encountering dangerous individuals.

- **Notable cases include Ashley Okland**, who was killed while working at an open house, and Beverly Carter, who was abducted and murdered while showing a property. These tragic incidents highlight the significant risks that female real estate agents may face.

- **Statistics and Safety Measures:** According to the National Association of Realtors, 73% of real estate professionals have reported fearing for their safety at some point during the past year, and many have been victims of crimes such as robberies and assaults during property showings.

In response, many real estate agents now carry self-defense weapons or utilize safety apps to track their whereabouts and alert colleagues in the event of an emergency.

RIP Sisters!

Name	Year	Location	Incident Summary
Patricia Whitmore	1983	New York, NY	Murdered during open house by a man posing as buyer
Betty "Betsy" Lou Ross	1989	Michigan	Abducted and killed by a prospective buyer
Sarah Walker	2006	Texas	Murdered in the open house, the attacker had no property ties
Lindsay Buziak	2008	Victoria, BC (Canada)	Killed during a showing; the case remains unsolved
Ann Nelson	2010	Des Moines, IA	Murdered by client at a property showing
Ashley Oakland	2011	Iowa	Fatally shot during an open house; unsolved
Beverly Carter	2014	Arkansas	Kidnapped/murdered at a fake showing led to new safety laws
Monique Baugh	2019	Minneapolis, MN	Lured to a show house, abducted, and murdered
Toni-Ann Byfield	2020	Miami, FL	Shot and killed while showing a home

4 years ago today, they found the body of REALTOR Beverly Carter. She went to work to meet a buyer, just like any other day. Except this "buyer" wasn't really a Buyer and instead made her a victim of a violent death. When a REALTOR asks you for your ID and a pre-qualification from a trusted lender, she is why they do it. Please oblige and don't take it personally. It's an extra layer of precaution amongst other things. Remember that your REALTOR is only human and is vulnerable to crime in their job. Beverly Carter Foundation

R.I.P.
Beverly Carter
REALTOR®

As we cope with our tragic loss, we ask the public to understand and respect our efforts to ensure our personal safety. This may include requiring you to meet with us at our office and/or requesting proof of your identification prior to showing you a home.
– Agents everywhere

These cases have prompted an increased focus on safety practices, including conducting background checks on new clients, utilizing buddy systems during showings, and implementing technology for enhanced security. Real estate professionals must be vigilant and proactive in their safety measures.

Finally, my mom was a Nurse Manager for a 75-bed OBGYN floor in the inner city of Hartford, CT, for over 30 years. During the 1970s and 1980s, she had to beg for security for her nurses in the parking lots at shift changes (11 pm - 7 am) as they were being attacked while getting into their cars.

Workplace violence tends to concentrate in high-stress, high-contact professions where employees interact with individuals in crisis or with authority over others' needs:

- **Healthcare (Hospitals, Emergency Departments, Behavioral Clinics):** Staff face verbal and physical aggression from patients under pain, intoxication, or psychiatric distress, especially in ERs and psychiatric units where de-escalation is critical.

- **Education (Schools and Universities):** Teachers and support personnel confront student outbursts, youth disputes, and unauthorized intruders — often at entry points, in hallways, and during disciplinary situations.

- **Public Sector (Municipal Offices, Social Services):** Front-line public employees (e.g., social workers, clerks) handle sensitive cases, such as child welfare and benefits appeals, where frustrated or desperate clients may lash out at counters or in waiting areas.

- **Veterans' Care (VHA Facilities):** Providers treating trauma-affected or mentally ill veterans encounter aggression during intake, exam rooms, and waiting areas as patients struggle with PTSD, substance misuse, or disability frustrations.

In each setting, violence stems from a combination of emotional distress, unmet needs, and power imbalances, underscoring the need for risk assessment, training in de-escalation, and targeted security measures in the most vulnerable locations.

Several organizations and states have implemented successful workplace violence prevention policies that have proven effective in reducing incidents and protecting employees. These examples highlight how comprehensive and well-enforced strategies can make a significant impact:

1. Healthcare Workers (Kaiser Permanente's Workplace Violence Prevention Program)

At Kaiser Permanente, frontline healthcare staff—particularly those in high-stress environments, such as emergency departments—benefit from a zero-tolerance policy for violence, combined with targeted risk assessments. By investing in de-escalation and conflict-resolution training, installing panic buttons and surveillance, and reinforcing secure entry systems, the program empowered nurses, technicians, and physicians to recognize warning signs early and respond safely. As a result, violent incidents dropped significantly, and staff reported greater confidence and peace of mind while delivering patient care.

2. Healthcare Employers & Staff (California's Cal/OSHA Violence Prevention Law)

California's landmark regulation requires every healthcare facility, from large hospitals to small clinics, to tailor its annual violence-risk assessments and prevention plans to its unique environment.

Mandatory training on warning-sign recognition, reporting protocols, and de-escalation techniques ensures that doctors, nurses, support staff, and administrators all speak the same safety language. Rigorous incident-tracking and enforcement have driven down workplace assaults statewide and fostered a culture of vigilance and accountability across the sector.

3. Teachers and School Personnel (NYC DOE Anti-Violence Initiative)

In New York City schools, educators and support staff encounter a range of aggression from students and visitors daily. The DOE's initiative equips teachers with crisis-intervention training. It establishes clear reporting channels while enhancing physical security using metal detectors, secure vestibules, and on-site officers at the highest-risk campuses.

By combining procedural safeguards with staff empowerment, the policy curbed violent incidents, improved response times, and uplifted teachers' sense of safety in the classroom.

4. Behavioral Health & Emergency Department Teams (UTMB's BERT Program)

Within the high-intensity setting of an academic medical center, psychiatric and emergency-care workers pioneered UTMB's Behavioral Emergency Response Team (BERT). BERT's specially trained responders and real-time monitoring tools mean staff never face a volatile patient alone.

Regular drills and de-escalation simulations keep everyone ready to intervene safely, from nurses to security personnel. The result: sharp declines in staff assaults and a replicable blueprint for other hospitals grappling with behavioral emergencies.

5. Public Sector Employees (Massachusetts Public Employees Act)

Teachers, healthcare aides, and municipal workers across Massachusetts now operate under a state law that mandates local risk assessments and customized violence-prevention plans.

Public-sector employers—from school districts to mental health clinics—must track every incident, invest in staff training, and secure facilities against potential threats. This legislative framework has driven down assault rates in schools and public offices alike, proving that data-driven policy and dedicated resources can protect the workforce in any government setting.

6. Veterans Health Administration (VHA Workplace Violence Prevention Program)

At VHA medical centers, where care providers often treat veterans with complex behavioral health needs, "disruptive behavior committees" review incidents and tailor interventions to each facility.

Clinicians, nurses, and support staff receive specialized training in managing aggression and early-warning protocols, supported by enhanced physical safeguards in exam rooms and waiting areas. Across the VHA network, these measures have reduced violent encounters and strengthened staff confidence in serving the veteran population.

These examples demonstrate that successful policies often include risk assessment, employee training, physical security enhancements, and transparent procedures for reporting and response.

By tailoring these elements to specific workplace environments and ensuring vigorous enforcement, organizations and states have been able to reduce workplace violence and protect employees effectively.

Simple Safety Recommendations for Business Professionals are encouraged to adopt several safety measures:

- **Use Safety Apps**: Tools like GPS Phone Track, Agent Safe Walk, and others can help agents stay connected with colleagues and alert authorities if they feel threatened.
- **Carry Self-Defense Tools**: Many agents carry pepper spray, personal alarms, or other self-defense tools.
- **Work in Pairs:** Whenever possible, showing properties with a partner can reduce the risk of being targeted.
- **Maintain Situational Awareness**: Remain vigilant about one's surroundings and have a plan for various scenarios.

Perilous Paths of Traveling in a Male Corporate World

Harassment, Discrimination, & Inadequate Infrastructure

Between the 1950s and the 1990s, business travel for women was fraught with numerous challenges and potential dangers, reflecting the broader societal attitudes and structural limitations of the time. Women often faced significant harassment and discrimination, both in the workplace and while traveling, compounded by a lack of safety-focused infrastructure and limited resources.

Cultural norms and workplace expectations added further pressure, while technological limitations hindered effective communication and access to information. Despite these obstacles, significant improvements have been made, enhancing safety and support for women travelers. This chapter explores the historical challenges faced by women in business travel and the advancements that have since transformed their travel experiences.

Safety Concerns in the 1950s - 1990s

- **Harassment and Discrimination:** Women often face significant sexual harassment, both in the workplace and while traveling, including unwanted advances from colleagues, clients, and strangers.
    - Discrimination was expected, with women frequently encountering gender bias and not being taken seriously in professional settings.

- **Lack of Infrastructure:** Many business hotels and accommodations were not designed with women's safety in mind, lacking essential security features such as well-lit parking lots, secure room access, and female-only floors.
  - Transportation options were limited, and there were no ride-sharing services, making it difficult for women to ensure safe travel to and from meetings or events.

- **Limited Resources and Support**: More resources and support networks are needed, specifically for women travelers.
  - The internet was not widely accessible, and mobile phones were not yet commonplace, limiting immediate access to help or information. Safety advice and travel tips were less comprehensive and less widely disseminated than they are today.

Cultural and Societal Barriers

- **Cultural Norms**: In many regions, traditional gender roles were more pronounced, making it difficult for women to travel alone without facing societal judgment or restrictions.

- Legal and cultural barriers in some countries restricted women's freedom of movement and behavior, increasing the risks associated with solo travel.

- **Workplace Expectations:** Women in business were often expected to prove themselves in male-dominated environments, leading to additional stress and pressure while traveling.
  - The lack of female mentors and role models in the corporate world meant that women often had to navigate these challenges without guidance or support.

Technological Limitations

- **Communication Barriers:** The absence of mobile phones and the internet meant that women needed more means of staying connected with their office or family while traveling.
  - Emergency assistance was more challenging to access, and coordination for travel plans was more cumbersome and less secure.

- **Limited Information**: Information about safe travel practices, particularly for women, was scarce.

- Guidebooks and travel agencies were the primary sources of information, which were not always up-to-date or comprehensive regarding safety concerns.

Improvements Over Time

- **Enhanced Security Measures:** Hotels and transportation services have implemented improved security practices, including accommodations that cater to female travelers.
- **Increased Awareness:** There is a greater awareness and reporting of harassment and discrimination, resulting in improved policies and practices.
- **Technological Advancements:** Mobile phones, the internet, and GPS have revolutionized travel safety, providing real-time information and support.
- **Support Networks:** Numerous organizations and online platforms now offer women travelers resources, tips, and community support.

Continued Progress in the 2000s, 2010s, and 2020s

- 2000s: The turn of the century brought significant advancements in communication technology, making mobile phones and internet access more widespread.

This era witnessed the emergence of online travel resources, safety apps, and more robust support networks. Business travel began to accommodate women more effectively, with improvements in hotel security and corporate policies addressing harassment and discrimination.

- 2010s: The rise of social media and movements like #MeToo brought unprecedented attention to the issues of sexual harassment and assault.

  Companies began implementing stricter anti-harassment policies, and travel services offered enhanced safety features. The decade also saw the development of sophisticated travel safety apps and GPS-based services, further improving the safety of women travelers.

- 2020s: The COVID-19 pandemic introduced new challenges and spurred innovations in virtual support and telecommuting options, reducing the need for travel.

As remote work has become more common, the focus has shifted to ensuring women's safety in digital spaces. The continued advocacy for women's rights and safety remains crucial, especially amid ongoing political and social changes.

Travel for women, both within the United States and abroad, has undergone significant evolution over the past few decades, reflecting shifts in safety, accommodation options, resources, and cultural awareness.

In the U.S., enhanced public transportation and accommodations safety measures, including safety features in ride-sharing services and women-only hotel floors, have contributed to a more secure travel environment. Online platforms and travel apps provide valuable resources and support, creating communities and networks for solo female travelers.

Internationally, improved tourism infrastructure, specific safety advisories for women, and a greater emphasis on cultural awareness have made travel more accessible and safer.

Mobile technology and social media offer constant connectivity and real-time assistance, enhancing the sense of community and security for women travelers when available.

Still, challenges such as harassment, cultural restrictions, and economic barriers persist, underscoring the importance of women remaining informed and cautious. By leveraging technology, understanding cultural norms, and connecting with support networks, women can enhance their travel experiences and navigate the complexities of solo travel more effectively.

There are many places in the world where I would not ask a woman analyst to help a client, such as in many parts of the United States, the Middle East, South America, and others. I have many stores about this subject.

Travel for women, both within the United States and internationally, has undergone significant changes over the past few decades. Here are some key developments and considerations:

United States

- **Safety and Security:** Increased awareness and measures have been implemented to enhance the safety of women in public transportation and accommodations. Ride-sharing services like Uber and Lyft have incorporated safety features, including GPS tracking, emergency buttons, and driver background checks. Airports and major transit hubs have enhanced security screening processes and increased the visibility of security personnel.

- **Accommodation Options:** The rise of women-only floors in hotels and women-friendly hostels provides safer and more comfortable lodging options. Online platforms like Airbnb offer more personalized and potentially safer accommodation choices, though carefully reviewing hosts and reading reviews is essential.

- **Resources and Support:** Numerous travel apps and websites offer safety tips, forums, and networks for solo women travelers. The Women's Travel Club and Pink Pangea provide community support and advice, as well as organize group trips for women.

International

- **Safety Precautions:** Many countries have enhanced their tourism infrastructure to cater to solo female travelers, with increased security in popular tourist destinations. International travel advisories often include specific advice for women, highlighting safer or more risky areas.

- **Cultural Awareness:** There is a growing emphasis on cultural awareness and sensitivity. Numerous resources are available to help women understand local customs and laws, which can impact their safety and comfort. Guides and blogs written by female travelers offer valuable insights into navigating different cultural landscapes safely.

- **Technology and Connectivity:** Mobile technology allows constant connectivity, providing access to maps, emergency contacts, and real-time updates on safety conditions. However, it is not always reliable. Social media platforms enable women to connect with other travelers and locals, offering a sense of community and immediate assistance if needed.

- **Legal and Regulatory Changes:** Visa regulations and travel restrictions can vary significantly, impacting how women travel to certain countries. Some regions have made it easier for solo travelers to obtain visas and navigate border controls. Health and safety regulations have become stricter, particularly following the COVID-19 pandemic, with a focus on hygiene and safety protocols in public spaces and transportation.

Challenges

- **Harassment and Assault:** Women may still face harassment and gender-based violence, especially in regions with less stringent laws protecting women's rights.

- **Cultural Restrictions:** In some countries, cultural norms and legal restrictions can limit women's freedom to travel alone or dictate specific behaviors and dress codes.

- **Economic Barriers:** The cost of travel can be significant, and women often need to be more cautious about budgeting for safety measures, such as staying in reputable accommodations and using secure transportation.

While travel for women, both domestically and internationally, has become more accessible and safer in many ways, it remains essential for women to stay informed, prepared, and cautious.

Leveraging technology, understanding cultural norms, and connecting with support networks can significantly enhance the travel experience for solo women travelers.

Women are VERY Fearful

Roots of Fear, Urgent Need for Cultural and Social Reforms.

Women today often experience a heightened sense of fear due to a combination of social and psychological factors. Historical and ongoing threats of violence, personal experiences, and social conditioning contribute to this pervasive fear, as women have been conditioned to be cautious to avoid becoming victims of male violence. Trust issues further exacerbate this fear, as the intentions of unknown men are seen as unpredictable and potentially dangerous.

Cultural narratives and media representations also amplify these fears by frequently highlighting stories of male-perpetrated violence. This complex interplay of factors is vividly illustrated in the current social media discussion about whether women prefer to encounter a bear or an unknown man in the woods. This hypothetical scenario, which has garnered significant attention on platforms like TikTok, underscores the deep-seated fears many women have regarding male violence. It highlights the need for societal changes to address and reduce gender-based violence, ensuring women's safety and security in all aspects of life.

Women today often feel a heightened sense of fear due to a variety of social and psychological factors. Studies and social discussions reveal several reasons why women might feel this way and why some even choose hypothetical scenarios involving dangerous animals over encounters with unknown men.

Reasons for Increased Fear:

- **Ongoing Threat of Violence:** Women have long been conditioned to be wary of potential violence from men due to high rates of domestic violence, sexual assault, and harassment. This historical context contributes to an ingrained sense of caution and fear.

- **Personal Experiences and Social Conditioning:** Many women have personal or second-hand experiences of male violence, which reinforces the fear of unknown men. Social conditioning teaches women to be vigilant and cautious to avoid becoming victims.

- **Trust Issues:** There is a general mistrust of unknown men because a bear's intentions are perceived as straightforward and predictable, whereas a man's intentions are seen as uncertain and potentially dangerous.

- **Cultural Narratives and Media Representation:** The Media often highlight stories of male-perpetrated violence, which can amplify fears. These narratives contribute to a culture where women feel constantly on guard against potential threats from men.

The current discussion about whether women would prefer to encounter a bear or an unknown man in the woods highlights the deep-seated fears many women have regarding male violence.

This hypothetical scenario, which has garnered significant attention and responses on social media platforms like TikTok, reveals that many women feel safer facing a bear because the animal's behavior is seen as predictable compared to the potential threat posed by a man. The bear is perceived as a straightforward danger, whereas an unknown man represents an unpredictable risk of violence, harassment, or assault. This choice underscores the extent of distrust and fear that women harbor due to personal experiences and societal conditioning, where the potential for male violence is ever-present.

The widespread resonance of this hypothetical question, which was explored through a series of interviews and discussions on social media, highlights the urgent need for societal changes to address and reduce gender-based violence and ensure women's safety and security in all aspects of life.

The fear many women experience today is a complex interplay of personal experiences, social conditioning, and cultural narratives. It underscores the broader issue of gender-based violence and the need for societal changes to ensure women feel safe and secure in their daily lives.

TRAUMA RESPONSES

FLIGHT	FIGHT
Workaholic	Anger outburst
Over-thinker	Controlling
Anxiety, panic, OCD	"The bully"
Difficulty sitting still	Narcissistic
Perfectionist	Explosive behaviour

FREEZE	FAWN
Difficulty making decisions	People pleaser
Stuck	Lack of identity
Dissociation	No boundaries
Isolating	Overwhelmed
Numb	Codependent

@RYANTHEHOLISTICHEALTHCOACH

Use Fear for Survival

One of my favorite books is "The Gift of Fear: Survival Signals That Protect Us from Violence" by Gavin de Becker, which emphasizes the importance of trusting one's instincts and intuition as powerful tools for personal safety. Here are the key takeaways and learnings from the book:

- **Trust Your Instincts:** De Becker argues that intuition is a powerful survival mechanism that can protect us from harm. He stresses the importance of listening to gut feelings and internal warnings, as these are often based on subtle cues that our subconscious picks up on.

- **Understanding Fear:** Fear is a natural and valuable emotion that signals danger. The book teaches readers to distinguish between genuine fear—a response to immediate threats—and unwarranted anxiety—a response to perceived, but not confirmed, threats.

- **Pre-Incident Indicators:** De Becker identifies behaviors and signals often preceding violence, such as forced teaming, charm, and excessive detail. Recognizing these pre-incident indicators can help individuals identify and avoid potentially dangerous situations.

- **Survival Signals:** The book outlines specific signals and behaviors that can alert someone to danger.
    - **Forced Teaming:** An attempt to create a false sense of unity or partnership.
    - **Charm and Niceness:** Used manipulatively to disarm and gain trust.
    - **Too Many Details:** Over-explaining to convince someone of something untrue.
    - **Typecasting:** Using a slight insult to make someone prove their worth.
    - **Loan Sharking**: Offering unsolicited help to create a sense of obligation.
    - **The Unsolicited Promise:** Promising something without being asked, often to gain trust.
    - **Discounting the Word "No":** Not accepting boundaries is a major red flag.

- **Real-Life Examples:** The book features numerous real-life examples and case studies that illustrate how intuition and awareness have saved lives. These stories reinforce the practical application of the concepts discussed.

"The Gift of Fear" is a powerful reminder that our intuition and instincts are crucial tools for survival. By learning to trust and act on these internal signals, individuals can better protect themselves from violence and harm. De Becker's insights into the behaviors that precede violence, along with his practical advice for personal safety, make this book an essential read for anyone interested in improving their situational awareness and security.

Empowerment Requires Mental & Physical Self-Defense Training

Address Societal Gaps in Training & Survival Skills

Traditional self-defense training often focuses on physical combat, which can be less effective for women facing stronger male attackers. These classes may overlook real-world scenarios that require situational awareness and psychological readiness, both of which are crucial for actual encounters.

Additionally, limited self-defense training can create a false sense of security, leading individuals to take unnecessary risks.

In contrast, survival training encompasses a broader range of skills, including situational awareness, risk avoidance, and emergency planning, which are essential for overall safety.

Societal Failures in Training Women

- **Cultural Norms**: From a young age, girls are socialized to be passive and non-confrontational, often prioritizing politeness and compliance over assertiveness. This socialization can hinder their ability to defend themselves effectively in dangerous situations.

- **Education:** Schools and educational programs rarely include self-defense or survival training in their curricula. Physical education typically emphasizes traditional sports over practical self-defense skills, leaving girls without essential tools for personal safety.

- **Access and Encouragement**: Women may face fewer opportunities to engage in self-defense training due to societal discouragement, financial barriers, and a lack of accessible programs. These obstacles perpetuate the notion that women are incapable of defending themselves.

- **Victim-Blaming**: Society often focuses on what women should do to avoid being attacked, such as not walking alone at night, rather than empowering them with skills to protect themselves in any situation. This shifts the responsibility onto women to avoid dangerous situations instead of addressing the root causes of violence.

- **Media Representation:** The Media frequently portrays women as victims rather than capable defenders. This lack of positive representation can impact women's perceptions of their abilities and erode their confidence in handling challenging situations.

Improving Training for Women

- **Early Education**: Incorporating self-defense and situational awareness training into school curricula can help build these essential skills from a young age, empowering girls to protect themselves effectively.

- **Positive Role Models**: Highlighting stories and media portrayals of women successfully defending themselves can inspire and empower others, showing that women can effectively protect themselves.

- **Accessible Programs:** Offering self-defense programs that are affordable and inclusive for all women can increase participation and ensure that more women can learn these vital skills.
- **Supportive Environment:** Encouraging a culture that supports and values training for women can help break down stereotypes and societal norms that discourage such training, fostering a more inclusive and empowering environment.

Physical Education and Sports

- **Gender Stereotypes:** Physical education often reinforces traditional gender roles, with boys encouraged to participate in competitive and aggressive sports while girls are steered towards less intense activities. This can limit girls' opportunities to develop strength and confidence.

- **Unequal Opportunities:** Girls require more opportunities and encouragement to participate in sports, which can lead to lower physical fitness and self-esteem. This disparity can perpetuate the notion that girls' physical prowess is less important.

- **Body Image Issues:** The societal focus on physical appearance can impact girls more severely, leading to self-consciousness and a reluctance to engage in physical activities fully. Boys are generally encouraged to value strength and athleticism more, positively influencing their engagement in sports.

- **Lack of Role Models:** The scarcity of female role models in many sports can discourage girls from participating. Conversely, boys often see numerous male athletes celebrated in the media, boosting their involvement and confidence.

- **Perceived Physical Abilities:** Girls may internalize societal messages that they are less capable physically, which can affect their performance and participation in sports. In contrast, boys often receive reinforcement for their physical abilities, which boosts their confidence and engagement.

Recommendations for Improvement

- **Inclusive Curriculum**: Develop a physical education curriculum that promotes equality, encouraging both boys and girls to participate in a range of activities.

- **Encourage Participation:** Actively support and encourage girls to engage in sports from a young age, providing equal resources and opportunities.

- **Positive Role Models:** Highlight and celebrate female athletes to provide positive role models for girls, showing them that they can succeed in sports.

- **Body Positivity**: Foster a positive body image environment that emphasizes health and fitness over appearance, helping all students feel confident and motivated to participate in physical activities.

By addressing these issues, physical education can become a more inclusive and empowering experience for all students. It can help break down gender barriers and promote equal participation, bridging the Gap Between Self-Defense Training and Survival Skills to create a safer, More Confident Society.

Another one of my favorite books is Meditations on Violence: A Comparison of Martial Arts Training and Real-World Violence" by Rory Miller.

It discusses the gaps between martial arts training and the realities of actual violence. Miller, a seasoned corrections officer and martial artist, offers a comprehensive analysis of the psychological and physical aspects of violent encounters. He emphasizes the differences between dojo training and real-world situations, offering practical advice on how to respond to threats effectively.

The book covers topics such as attackers' mindsets, the effects of adrenaline, and the importance of situational awareness. It's a critical read for anyone interested in realistic self-defense training. What did I learn?

- **The Difference Between Training and Reality:** Traditional martial arts training often fails to simulate the unpredictability and chaos of real-world violence. Real encounters are more sudden, intense, and unstructured.

- **Mindset and Psychology:** Understanding attackers' mindsets and recognizing the effects of adrenaline are crucial. Mental preparation and situational awareness can be as important as physical skills.

- **Adaptability:** Techniques practiced in a controlled environment may need to be adapted or abandoned in a real fight. Flexibility and improvisation are key.

- **Realistic Training:** Incorporating scenario-based training that mimics real-life situations can better prepare individuals for actual confrontations.

- **Legal and Ethical Considerations**: Knowing the legal implications of self-defense actions and the ethical boundaries is essential. Understanding when and how to use force appropriately is also critical to self-defence.

These lessons emphasize the importance of realistic training and mental preparedness for effectively handling real-world violence. I suggest you look for realistic training scenarios at www.rad-systems.com, which offers training across the US and Canada.

Other Books and Resources on Self-Defense and Empowerment for Women

- **The New Superpower for Women**: Trust Your Intuition, Predict Dangerous Situations, and Defend Yourself from the Unthinkable, by Steve Kardian, teaches practical self-defense techniques to women, helping them harness their intuition.
- **When Violence Is the Answer**: Learning How to Do What It Takes When Your Life Is at Stake, by Tim Larkin, explores the mindset and techniques necessary for practical self-defence.

Online Resources

- **National Self-Defense Institute**: Provides self-defense and personal safety training and resources.
- **RAINN (Rape, Abuse & Incest National Network):** Offers information and support for victims of sexual violence.

These books and resources provide valuable insights into self-defence, situational awareness, and the psychological aspects of staying safe. They can help women build confidence and practical skills to protect themselves.

Avoiding Abduction

Be Alert, Stay Safe, and Prevent Dangerous Situations

Abduction is not just a standalone crime; it frequently precedes other severe offenses, making its prevention and immediate counteraction crucial for personal safety.

Many defense strategies are specifically designed to avoid or escape abduction scenarios, which are particularly relevant to women, as such strategies are generally less applicable to men.

Abduction can be defined as the act of forcibly taking someone away against their will.

This act not only restricts a person's freedom of movement but also creates a perilous situation where the victim is isolated and under the control of the abductor.

The methods used in abduction typically include:
- physical force
- threats of violence
- or psychological intimidation
- all aimed at overpowering the victim and preventing escape.

From a legal standpoint, abduction is treated as a severe crime (Felony) due to its implications and the potential for subsequent criminal activities, such as assault, sexual violence, or murder.

The crime of abduction, classified as a felony, often involves the unlawful restraint of a person's freedom of movement through force, threat, or intimidation.

In many jurisdictions, the legal system imposes harsh penalties on those convicted of abduction to deter such crimes and protect potential victims. Understanding the legal definitions and implications of abduction is crucial for recognizing the seriousness of the threat and the importance of taking defensive measures.

Avoiding abduction is a critical aspect of self-defence, as it significantly reduces the risk of further violence and harm. Once abducted, an individual loses control and faces heightened danger in isolated locations.

We need to emphasize that situational awareness, early escape, and effective self-defense techniques are among the most crucial measures for preventing abduction. By understanding and implementing these strategies, individuals can enhance their safety and be better prepared to respond to potential threats, ensuring they remain in control and minimize the risks associated with dangerous situations.

Avoiding Abduction is Key to Safety and Defense

- **Situational Awareness:** Remaining aware of your surroundings is crucial for avoiding abduction. This involves being vigilant, especially in unfamiliar or isolated areas.

- **Trust your instincts:** if something feels off, it probably is. Being observant and mindful can help you recognize potential threats early and take pre-emptive action to avoid danger.

- **Avoid Routine:** Predictability can make you an easier target for someone planning an abduction. By varying your routines and routes, you make it more difficult for a potential attacker to anticipate your movements and plan an attack. This unpredictability can significantly reduce the risk of being targeted.

- **Escape Early:** The best time to escape is during the initial moments of an attack, when attackers are often least prepared for resistance. Use any available means to create a distraction, such as throwing objects or making sudden movements, to increase your chances of breaking free and getting away before the situation escalates.

- **Make Noise:** Making noise can attract attention and deter an attacker. Scream, use a personal alarm, or bang on objects to create loud noises. The goal is to alert others nearby to your distress and scare off the attacker, who might not want to be aware of their actions.

- **Fight Back:** If escape isn't immediately possible, using 120% of your effort and techniques to fight back can be crucial. Target vulnerable areas of the attacker, such as the eyes, nose, throat, and groin, to inflict pain and create an opportunity to escape. Self-defense and situational training can help you learn how to handle such violent attacks.

- Implementing these strategies can enhance personal safety and reduce the likelihood of abduction. Staying aware, being prepared to escape or fight back, making noise, and avoiding predictable patterns are all essential elements of a robust self-defense plan.

I Fight Like a Girl

With a sense of anger and an unwavering will to fight
back fiercely in a life-or-death struggle:

I fight like a girl, with fury unchained,
With fists that won't falter, with blood in my veins.
I am rage in the darkness, a storm that won't break,

For I'll fight to the death – I'm no easy take.

I fight like a girl, every breath charged with fire,
With wrath in my heart, with vengeance inspired.
I will claw, I will bite, I will tear to be free,
And death stands beside me, unyielding as I am.

I fight like a girl, and I won't go unheard,
With screams that cut deep, as sharp as my words.
My anger's my armor; my pulse beats like war,
I won't stop till I've won, till I'm safe, till you're gone.

I fight like a girl, with all that I am,
With power that terrifies, that no one can damn.
So if you come for me, know I'll answer with wrath,

For I fight like a girl – and I'll fight to the last.

Source: Circulates online as an anonymous or user-generated piece.
There's no known author, publisher, or first appearance in a
recognized collection.

The Mind of Predators

Recognize and Avoid Dangerous People

Predatory behavior is far more common than most people realize: studies estimate that one in five women and one in seventy-one men will experience sexual assault in their lifetime, and roughly 90% of those perpetrators are known friends, intimate partners, or acquaintances, rather than strangers!

Predators often scout for vulnerability, targeting those who appear isolated, distracted, or emotionally distressed. They move quickly—sometimes befriending a victim online or in person within hours—and employ tactics such as feigned sympathy, charm, or "tests" of trust to lower their victim's defenses.

While violent assaults grab headlines, most predator attacks involve gradual emotional manipulation, making early recognition of grooming behaviors (excessive flattery, unsolicited gifts, boundary-pushing questions) and situational red flags (requests for secrecy, attempts to isolate) critical.

By understanding that predatory tactics can unfold in minutes or span weeks—and that opportunistic predators look for both physical and online openings—women can stay more vigilant, trust their instincts, and employ protective strategies like setting firm boundaries, maintaining public meeting places, and using trusted "check-ins" with friends or family to disrupt a predator's plans before they escalate.

Predators use manipulative and deceptive tactics to target vulnerable individuals, making it essential to understand their behaviors and strategies.

The statistic that "more than 2 million women are assaulted every year" might have been relevant in the past. Still, current data suggests that the number of women experiencing intimate partner violence and sexual assault annually in the U.S. is significantly higher when considering physical assaults alongside sexual assaults.

Many incidents go unreported, making it challenging to determine the exact number of assaults. Here's a more current understanding of the issue:

- **Intimate Partner Violence:** The National Center for Injury Prevention and Control indicates that women experience about **4.8 million** intimate partner-related physical assaults and rapes every year.[1]

- **Lifetime Prevalence:** Approximately 1 in 5 (21.3% or an estimated **25.5 million**) women in the U.S. report experiencing completed or attempted rape at some point in their lifetime.

- **Broader Context:** Every year, nearly 10 million women and men become victims of domestic violence in the United States. Intimate partner violence accounts for 15% of all violent crime.

Let's examine the profiles, motivations, and methods of common predators, including their strategies for selecting and hunting victims. By recognizing these patterns and implementing proactive safety measures, women can significantly reduce their risk of becoming targets.

Tim Larkin, author of "Survive the Unthinkable: A Total Guide to Women's Self-Protection, believes that traditional self-defense training for women is not enough because it often focuses solely on physical techniques without addressing the broader context of violence and the mindset needed to prevent and respond to it effectively.**

Here are some key reasons he provides, along with insights into the alarming statistics:

- **Mindset and Preparedness:** Larkin emphasizes that physical techniques alone are insufficient without the right mindset. Women need to be mentally prepared to recognize and react to threats before they escalate to physical violence.

  - **Insight:** Many women are not taught to trust their instincts or to be assertive in setting and maintaining boundaries, leaving them vulnerable to escalating situations.

- **Comprehensive Awareness**: Effective self-defense requires situational awareness and the ability to recognize and avoid potentially hazardous situations.

  - **Insight:** Traditional self-defense classes often need more time to teach women to be constantly aware of their surroundings and identify potential threats early.

- **Understanding the Attacker's Mindset:** Larkin stresses the importance of understanding how attackers think and operate. This knowledge can help women anticipate and thwart potential attacks.
  - **Insight:** Without this understanding, women may not fully grasp the importance of early intervention and proactive measures to prevent an attack.

- **Behavioral Strategies**: Beyond physical defense, women must know how to use behavioral strategies to de-escalate or avoid confrontations.

  - **Insight:** Many training programs fail to cover verbal and non-verbal communication skills, which can help diffuse a potential attack before it escalates into physical violence.

- **Realistic Training Scenarios:** Larkin advocates for realistic training that simulates attack scenarios, helping women build the confidence and experience to respond effectively.

  - Insight: Traditional self-defense classes often use controlled environments that do not accurately replicate the stress and unpredictability of real-life attacks.

- **Statistical Reality:** The statistics highlight the pervasive nature of violence against women and the need for a more holistic approach to self-protection.

  - **Insight:** This high rate of assault indicates that many women are not adequately prepared to prevent or defend against attacks, underscoring the need for comprehensive education on personal safety.

By addressing these broader issues, Tim Larkin believes women can be better equipped to defend themselves physically, prevent and respond to threats more effectively, and be empowered.

Understanding Predators: Who, What, Where, Why, and How They Hunt

Who They Are: Predators can come from any background, but often they share certain psychological traits such as narcissism, lack of empathy, and manipulative behavior. They may present themselves as charming or trustworthy to gain the trust of their victims. Predators include serial killers, sexual offenders, stalkers, and abusive partners, friends, or co-workers. Each type has distinct behaviors and methods for selecting and pursuing victims.

What They Do: Predators seek to exert control and dominance over their victims. This can manifest as physical violence, sexual assault, psychological manipulation, or stalking. They often use grooming techniques to build a sense of trust and dependence in their victims before attacking. This may involve flattery, gifts, or isolating the victim from their support network.

Where They Hunt: Predators can operate anywhere, but common hunting grounds include public places like bars and clubs, online platforms, workplaces, and even within the victim's home environment. They may frequent places where potential victims are likely to be alone or vulnerable, such as parking lots, parks, or secluded areas.

Why They Hunt: Predators' motivations can vary but often include a need for power, control, and gratification. Some may have deep-seated psychological issues or a history of abuse themselves. Many predators seek the thrill of the hunt and derive pleasure from the suffering of their victims. For some, the act of predation fulfills a compulsive need.

How They Hunt: Predators typically target and select victims who appear vulnerable, isolated, or easily manipulated. This could be someone physically weaker, emotionally distressed, looking at their phone, or lacking a solid support network. They often use a combination of charm, deceit, and coercion to lure their victims. Once the victim is isolated, the predator may use threats or physical force to maintain control.

Understanding the Mind of an Attacker

In "Survive the Unthinkable: A Total Guide to Women's Self-Protection," Tim Larkin explores the mindset of an attacker to help women better understand how to protect themselves. Here are some key insights, each accompanied by an example:

- **Predatory Nature:** Attackers often have a predatory mindset, seeking easy targets who appear vulnerable or distracted. For example, an attacker might target a woman engrossed in her phone while walking alone at night, perceiving her as less aware of her surroundings.

- **Opportunity and Control**: Attackers look for situations where they can exert control over their victims with minimal risk to themselves. For example, an attacker may wait in a secluded parking garage, knowing it's less likely that someone will intervene or witness the assault.

- **Dehumanization:** Many attackers dehumanize their victims to justify their actions, viewing them as objects rather than individuals with rights and feelings. For example, an attacker might rationalize their behavior by convincing themselves that the victim "deserved it" because of how they dressed or acted.

- **Testing Boundaries:** Attackers often test potential victims' boundaries before fully committing to an attack. For example, an attacker might make inappropriate comments or invade personal space to see if the woman resists or is too intimidated to respond.

- **Psychological Manipulation:** Attackers use psychological tactics to manipulate and intimidate their victims, instilling fear and compliance. For example, an attacker might threaten a woman with harm to her loved ones if she doesn't comply, creating fear and forcing her into submission.

- **Anticipation of Resistance:** While attackers prefer easy targets, they are also prepared for some level of resistance. For example, an attacker might carry a weapon or have a plan for quickly subduing a victim if she tries to fight back, underscoring the importance of being proactive and decisive in self-defence.

By understanding these aspects of an attacker's mindset, women can better recognize potential threats and take proactive steps to protect themselves. Larkin emphasizes the importance of awareness, setting boundaries, and assertiveness in countering attackers' strategies.

Avoidance Recommendations

These books provide numerous lessons and insights into predatory behavior, predator psychology, and methods for prevention and awareness. Here are the critical lessons learned from each book:

Survive the Unthinkable: A Total Guide to Women's Self-Protection" by Tim Larkin is a comprehensive resource dedicated to empowering women with the knowledge and skills necessary to protect themselves. The book emphasizes the importance of understanding your environment, identifying safe places and exits, and learning basic self-defense techniques that target vulnerable points on an attacker's body. Everyday objects can also be used effectively as safety tools.

Inside the Mind of a Predator: This book provides an in-depth look at the psychological, verbal, and physical tactics used by predators to target women. It includes prevention strategies and insights to help women recognize and avoid potentially dangerous situations.

The New Predator: Women Who Kill: Profiles of Female Serial Killers" by Deborah Schurman-Kauflin: Based on face-to-face interviews with female serial killers, this book highlights the psychological profiles and methods used by these women. It provides professionals and the public with valuable information on identifying warning signs and understanding the differences between male and female killers. The book also discusses how these women select their victims and their motivations for killing.

The Human Predator: A Historical Chronicle of Serial Murder and Forensic Investigation by Katherine Ramsland: Traces the history of serial killers and the evolution of forensic investigation. It offers insights into the minds of notorious killers and the methods used to track and capture them. The book provides a comprehensive overview of how predatory behaviors have been understood and investigated throughout history.

All the President's Women: Donald Trump and the Making of a Predator. This book details numerous allegations of sexual misconduct against Donald Trump, providing a broader context of how predatory behavior can manifest in positions of power. It includes interviews and behind-the-scenes reporting that shed light on the tactics and patterns of such predators.

General Lessons Across All Books:

- **Psychological Insights**: Gaining a deeper understanding of the psychological underpinnings of predatory behavior.
- **Behavioral Indicators**: Recognizing early warning signs and behavioral indicators of potential predators.
- **Importance of Education:** The crucial role of educating the public, especially vulnerable groups, on recognizing and preventing predatory behavior.
- **Support Systems**: Support systems for victims are needed, and providing resources and assistance to those affected by predatory actions is essential.

These books and resources offer valuable insights into predators' mindsets, enabling women to understand and protect themselves from potential dangers. They provide psychological perspectives and practical guidance on recognizing and responding to threats. You can find these books on platforms like Amazon, Goodreads, and various academic publishers.

GENERAL LESSONS ACROSS ALL BOOKS

PSYCHOLOGICAL INSIGHTS

Understand the psychology behind predatory behavior

BEHAVIORAL INDICATORS

Recognizing early warning signs and behavioral indicators

IMPORTANCE OF EDUCATION

The crucial role of educating public, especially vulnerable groups, on recognizing and preventing

SUPPORT SYSTEMS

Providing support systems and assistance to those affected by predatory actions

Seconds Matter

How Awareness, Preparation, and Swift Action Can Save Lives

Understanding the brain's response time in high-stress situations is crucial for implementing adequate safety and self-defense measures. While the brain can process information rapidly, various factors can delay immediate reactions.

The "3-second rule" emphasizes the need for quick assessment, decision-making, and action to ensure safety. Factors like cognitive load, stress responses, decision-making complexities, lack of experience, distractions, and physiological conditions can slow down the brain's response.

We encourage individuals to remain aware, prepared, and decisive, thereby reducing hesitation and enhancing their ability to protect themselves effectively. Being mentally prepared can significantly improve safety outcomes, whether assessing a threat, deciding on the best response, or taking swift action.

Various factors can influence the brain's response time, which can sometimes take up to three seconds. And in high-stress situations, several factors can affect response speed:

Cognitive Load: The brain must process significant information to assess a threat. This includes sensory input, memories, and potential outcomes, which can take time.

Stress Response: High-stress situations can trigger the fight-or-flight response, which sometimes causes a moment of freezing or indecision as the brain determines the best course of action.

Decision-Making: Evaluating options and choosing the best response involves complex neural processes. The brain must weigh the risks and benefits, which can slow down the immediate reaction.

Experience and Training: Individuals trained in self-defense or emergency response often react more quickly because their brains are conditioned to respond rapidly to specific stimuli. Lack of knowledge can lead to longer decision-making times.

- **Distraction and Situational Awareness:** If a person is distracted or unaware of their surroundings, recognizing a threat and responding accordingly can take longer.

- **Physiological Factors**: Fatigue, alcohol, drugs, or medical conditions can impair cognitive and motor functions, slowing response times.

The 3-second rule for safety and self-defense refers to the principle that, during a potentially dangerous or threatening situation, individuals should be able to assess, react, and move to a safer position within three seconds.

This rule emphasizes the importance of making quick decisions and taking immediate action to protect oneself. Here are the critical aspects of the 3-second rule:

- **Assessment**: Quickly evaluate the situation to understand the threat level. Look for potential escape routes, identify any immediate dangers, and decide on the best action.

- **Reaction**: Based on your assessment, decide how to respond. This may include relocating to a safer location, preparing to defend yourself, or employing verbal de-escalation techniques.

- **Action**: Execute your chosen response. This could involve moving away from the threat, using self-defense techniques, or calling for help.

It is essential to be aware of your surroundings and prepared to act swiftly in an emergency. This will reduce hesitation and ensure that individuals can protect themselves effectively in dangerous situations.

Always, always, trust your gut. If you feel something is wrong, that's because it usually is.

WomenWorking.com

Source: The graphic originated from WomenWorking.com, where it was published as part of their personal-safety and empowerment content.

"In the Blink of an Eye: 3 Seconds Can Change Your Life" by Jesse Blackadder offers advice and examples on safety and the importance of making quick decisions. While I can't provide specific excerpts from the book, I can summarize some of the general advice and types of examples that books on this topic typically include:

Advice

- **Stay Aware**: Always be mindful of your surroundings. Situational awareness is crucial in recognizing potential threats early.
- **Trust Your Instincts**: If something feels off, trust your gut feelings. Your intuition is often a valuable guide in dangerous situations.

- **Prepare Mentally and Physically**: Regularly consider potential scenarios and how you would react. Practice self-defense techniques and have a plan in place.

- **React Quickly but Calmly:** Take a moment to assess the situation in a crisis, then act decisively. Remaining calm can help you think more clearly and make better, more informed decisions.

- **Have a Plan:** Know your escape routes, safe places, and have contingency plans in place. Being prepared can make a significant difference in emergencies.

Practical Scenarios

- **Walking Alone at Night:** Advice on how to stay safe by choosing well-lit paths, avoiding distractions like headphones, and being aware of surroundings.

- **Driving:** Tips on defensive driving, including maintaining a safe distance, being vigilant for erratic drivers, and knowing how to respond to sudden hazards.

- **Home Safety**: Securing your home, including installing alarms, utilizing sturdy locks, and developing an emergency plan.

Emergency Responses

- **Fire Safety**: Knowing evacuation routes, having fire extinguishers readily available, and practicing fire drills are essential.

- **Medical Emergencies:** Guidance on quickly assessing and responding to medical emergencies, including CPR and first aid.

This advice and examples illustrate how a few seconds of quick thinking and preparation can significantly ensure safety and prevent harm.

Understanding the brain's response time in high-stress situations is crucial for implementing adequate safety and self-defense measures. Books and resources that delve into this topic provide valuable insights into quick decision-making, situational awareness, and practical self-defense strategies.

Finally, when reviewing **"Just 2 Seconds: Using Time and Space to Defeat Assassins and Other Adversaries**" by Gavin de Becker, Tom Taylor, and Jeff Marquart is a comprehensive guide on personal protection and threat management.

It emphasizes the critical moments leading up to an attack, highlighting the importance of a swift and immediate reaction to prevent harm. The book includes detailed analyses of numerous attacks, offering practical lessons for protectors and individuals on how to respond to imminent threats effectively. It is a valuable resource for anyone involved in security and threat assessment. https://just2seconds.org/

Sources:

"The Gift of Fear" by Gavin de Becker focuses on trusting intuition and recognizing warning signs to stay safe.

"In the Blink of an Eye: 3 Seconds" Can Change Your Life. Jesse Blackadder offers advice and examples on making quick decisions and prioritizing safety.

Understanding Self-Defense Laws

Navigate the Differences in Rights to Protect Yourself Effectively

Understanding your right to self-defense is crucial, particularly considering the complexities and variations in the law across different jurisdictions. Generally, self-defense laws allow you to protect yourself from imminent harm, but the specifics, such as the requirement to retreat or the extent of force that can be used, vary significantly by state or province.

Additionally, special considerations come into play in domestic violence situations, where the history of abuse and the ongoing nature of threats are critical factors.

Laws like the Violence Against Women Act (VAWA) provide further protections and support for victims of domestic violence and sexual assault. Knowing these laws and your rights can empower you to act confidently and appropriately in dangerous situations.

You have the right to defend yourself, which is generally recognized under self-defense laws. However, the specifics of this right can vary by jurisdiction.

Section 1: Principles of Self-Defense Law:

- **Reasonable Belief:** You must reasonably believe you are in imminent danger of harm or unlawful force. The threat must be present, immediate, and not based on a future or hypothetical scenario.

- **Proportional Response:** The force used in self-defense must be proportional to the threat. Excessive force beyond what is necessary to prevent harm can not be justified unless violent threats or abduction are occurring at that time.

- **Duty to Retreat (Varies by State):** Some states have a "duty to retreat" requirement, where you must attempt to avoid the confrontation if possible before using force. Other states have "Stand Your Ground" laws, which permit the use of force without retreating if you are lawfully present.

- **Castle Doctrine**: Many states have laws that extend the right to use force, including deadly force, to protect your home (the "castle doctrine"). This principle generally applies when someone unlawfully enters your home and poses a threat to your safety.

- **Defense of Others:** You can use reasonable force to defend others in imminent danger of harm. The same principles of reasonable belief and proportional response apply.

- **No Aggressor:** You cannot claim self-defense if you were the initial aggressor or provoked the confrontation. However, if you withdraw from the confrontation and communicate your intent to stop, and the other party continues to attack, you may regain the right to self-defense.

Example of Legal Text (Hypothetical State Law):

Use of Force in Defense of Person: A person is justified in using force against another when and to the extent that they reasonably believe it is necessary to defend themselves or a third person against the imminent use of unlawful force. A person may use deadly force if they reasonably believe it is required to prevent imminent death, serious bodily injury, kidnapping, or sexual assault.

- **Duty to Retreat**: A person is not required to retreat if they are in a place where they have a legal right to be. This section does not apply if the person using force is engaged in unlawful activity.

- **Defense of Dwelling:** A person is justified in using deadly force to defend their dwelling if they reasonably believe it is necessary to prevent or terminate an unlawful entry or attack. The use of force is presumed to be reasonable if the person against whom the force was used was in the process of unlawfully and forcibly entering or had unlawfully and forcibly entered the dwelling.

Key Differences in Domestic Situations:

- **Context and History:** In domestic violence cases, the history of abuse and the relationship between the parties involved can play a significant role in legal proceedings. Courts may consider patterns of abuse, past incidents, and the ongoing nature of the threat when evaluating self-defense claims.

- **Battered Woman Syndrome:** This is a psychological condition that can affect individuals who have been subjected to prolonged domestic abuse. It may be used in court to help explain why a person in a domestic violence situation believed they were in imminent danger and why their response was reasonable.

- **No Duty to Retreat:** In many jurisdictions, the "duty to retreat" requirement is relaxed or does not apply in one's home, which is often relevant in domestic violence cases. The "Castle Doctrine" typically supports the right to use force, including deadly force, without retreating when in your home.

- **Imminence of Threat:** The concept of imminent threat can be more nuanced in domestic violence cases. Courts may recognize that the threat does not need to be immediate in the same way as in other situations because of the ongoing nature of domestic abuse and the potential for future harm.

- **Protective Orders:** Violation of protective orders by the abuser can be a factor in self-defense claims. If an abuser violates a restraining order, the victim's use of force in response to perceived threats may be more easily justified.

- **Law Enforcement Response:** Police and courts often take domestic violence seriously and may have specialized units and protocols to handle these cases. This can affect the initial response, investigation, and legal proceedings.

- **Documentation:** Keeping records of past abuse, such as photographs, medical records, and police reports, can be crucial in supporting a self-defense claim in a domestic violence situation.

- **Witnesses:** Testimony from friends, family members, neighbors, or others who are aware of the abuse can be valuable in establishing the context of ongoing threats.

- **Seeking Help:** Victims of domestic violence are encouraged to seek help from shelters, support groups, and legal advocates. These resources can provide immediate safety and long-term support.

- **Legal Representation:** It's essential to have legal representation experienced in domestic violence cases. They can navigate the complexities of the law and ensure that the victim's rights and experiences are represented adequately in court.

Understanding the legal principles of self-defense is crucial, whether you are defending yourself or another person. Both scenarios require a reasonable belief in imminent danger and a proportional response to the threat. However, defending another person, especially a child, often invokes additional considerations due to vulnerability.

Jurisdictions vary on the duty to retreat, with some requiring it and others allowing the use of force without retreating if lawfully present. Familiarizing yourself with these laws ensures you can act appropriately in dangerous situations while remaining within legal boundaries.

Defending Another Person

When defending another person, you must reasonably believe they are in imminent danger of harm or unlawful force. The threat must be immediate and not based on a hypothetical scenario.

The force used to defend another must be proportional to the threat, meaning excessive force is unjustified. Some jurisdictions require an attempt to retreat before using force, while others do not. Special considerations apply when defending children, as they are more vulnerable and often warrant a higher duty of care.

- **Reasonable Belief:** You must reasonably believe that the person you defend is in imminent danger of harm or unlawful force. The threat must be immediate and not based on a future or hypothetical scenario.

- **Proportional Response:** The force used to defend another person must be proportional to the threat. Excessive force beyond what is necessary to prevent harm is generally not justified.

- **Duty to Retreat (Varies by Jurisdiction):**
  Some states require you to attempt to avoid
  the confrontation, if possible, before using
  force. In contrast, others allow you to use force
  without retreating if you are lawfully present.

- **Special Considerations for Children:**
  Defending a child often invokes a higher duty
  of care and may be more readily justified due
  to the child's vulnerability.

- **Defending Yourself:** In self-defence, you
  must reasonably believe you are in imminent
  danger of harm. The force must be
  proportional to the threat faced, avoiding
  excessive force. Jurisdictions vary on the duty
  to retreat, with some requiring it and others
  allowing you to stand your ground if lawfully
  present. The Castle Doctrine, applicable in
  many states, permits the use of force,
  including deadly force, to protect your home
  from unlawful entry and threats to your
  safety.

- **Proportional Response: Reasonable Belief:**
  You must reasonably believe you are in
  imminent danger of harm or unlawful force.
  The force used in self-defense must be
  proportional to the threat faced. Excessive
  force beyond what is necessary to prevent
  damage is not justified.

- **Duty to Retreat (Varies by Jurisdiction):** Like defending others, some states require a "duty to retreat," whereas others have "Stand Your Ground" laws that permit the use of force without retreating if you are lawfully present.

Examples of State Differences

- **California:** Has the Castle Doctrine and allows for consideration of BWS in self-defense claims. California law emphasizes the reasonableness of the belief that force was necessary.

- **Florida**: A prominent Stand Your Ground state, which means individuals do not have a duty to retreat anywhere they have a legal right to be.

- **New York:** Requires a duty to retreat if safely possible before using deadly force in self-defence, except in one's home.

Self-defense laws and their application in domestic violence situations can vary widely depending on the state or province.

Understanding the specific legal framework in your jurisdiction is essential. Individuals facing such situations should seek legal counsel to navigate these complex laws and protect their rights.

Here were some reliable sources for understanding self-defense laws, domestic violence considerations, and the Violence Against Women Act (VAWA): (DODJ might defund some)

Essential Safety Tips

Initiative-Taking Strategies for Staying Safe at Home, in Public, and Online

Ensuring personal safety is paramount for women today, whether at home, in public, or online. By adopting proactive strategies, women can significantly reduce their risk of encountering dangerous situations and enhance their overall sense of security.

This guide provides practical tips, ranging from maintaining situational awareness and securing one's home to traveling safely and using technology effectively. Empower yourself with these essential safety measures to stay protected and confident in all aspects of life.

General Safety Tips

Stay Aware of Your Surroundings
- **Be mindful** of who and what is around you.
- **Avoid distractions**, such as looking at your phone while walking, driving, or watching others.

- **Trust your instincts.** If something feels off, it probably is. Leave the area or seek help. This has saved my life several times.

Plan Your Route and Share Your Location

- **Plan your route ahead of time**, especially if you're traveling to an unfamiliar destination.
- **When walking or driving, use well-lit, busy streets.**
- When heading out alone, **share your location** or travel plans with a trusted friend or family member.
- Plan how to get to and from your destination and **tell others you've returned home.**
- **Do not have them pick you up,** especially if you go out at night and have not met the person a few times in Public.
- **Take your vehicle, Taxi, or Uber/Lift.**

Keep Emergency Contacts Handy

- **Save emergency contacts in your phone** and label them clearly.
- Consider having **a written list of emergency contacts in** your wallet, backpack, suitcase, and briefcase.

Self-Defense Training

- **Take a self-defense class** to learn how to protect yourself in case of an attack. Please practice the techniques. **www.rad-systems.com** or your local Martial Arts Studio
- **Take a refresher or regularly make sure you can perform** them effectively if needed.

At Home

- **Secure Your Home:** Always lock doors and windows, including those on the inside. If using screens, install metal guards.
- **Consider installing security systems,** including cameras and alarms. Put up signs to tell people you are using cameras so they will choose another location.
- **Use Peepholes and Intercoms:** Always check who is at the door before opening it. If available, use a peephole or intercom system. You do not have to open the door.
- **Emergency Plan:** Plan what to do in case of a break-in, including escape routes and safe places to hide.
- **Phone by your bed** if you need to call 911.
- **Keep your car keys by your bed** so you can set off the alarm.
- **Avoid posting details** about your location or travel plans on social media in real-time.

While Out and About

- **Walk with purpose and confidence.** Making eye contact can often deter someone with bad intentions.
- **If you feel uncomfortable,** don't hesitate to remove yourself from the situation or ask for help.
- **Travel in Groups:** Whenever possible, travel with friends or family, especially at night. Do NOT leave your group with someone you do not know. Use well-lit and populated routes.
- **Stay Sober and Alert**: Be cautious with alcohol, never leave your drink unattended, and be careful about accepting drinks from others.
- **If you feel unwell or suspect you've been drugged,** seek help immediately. Go to the Ladies' room or the host.
- **Plan to leave before the last call,** when predators hunt in the bar and parking lot. Please stay in the parking lot in your locked car until all your friends start their vehicles.
- **Use Public Transportation Safely: Wait in well-lit areas and near other people** when using public transportation. Sit near the driver or in populated sections of the vehicle.
- **Exercise caution when using rideshares or Public Transportation.** Use official taxis or rideshares and avoid walking alone in unfamiliar or unsafe areas.

- **Verify the identity of your driver** before getting into a rideshare vehicle. Check the car details and ask the driver for their name. Call someone and leave the information with them. Sit in the back seat and keep your belongings always close.
- **When traveling alone, keep your hotel room locked**, avoid sharing your room number publicly, and familiarize yourself with emergency exits.

In Your Vehicle

- **Car Safety:** Lock your doors when leaving or entering your car. Park in well-lit areas and avoid parking near large vehicles, Vans, or bushes where someone can hide.
- **Have an Emergency Kit:** Keep an emergency kit in your car with a flashlight, blanket, first-aid supplies, duct tape, tie wraps, and a phone charger.
- **Breakdown Protocol:** If your car breaks down, stay inside with the doors locked and call for help. If a stranger offers help, tell them you have called the police or a tow service unless your phone is not working. You only crack your window so they cannot get into the car.

Online Safety

- **Privacy Settings:** Use strong, unique passwords for all online accounts and change them regularly.
- **On social media, you can adjust privacy settings** to Friends, not Public, to limit who can see your information.
- **Be Cautious with Personal Information:** Avoid sharing too much personal information online.
- **Please be careful when accepting or making friend requests** from people you do not know.
- **Online Dating Safety:** Use reputable dating sites and apps. Could you arrange the first several meetings in public places and let someone know where you will be?
- **Be careful about sharing personal information** with strangers or on social media. Avoid disclosing details such as your home address or daily routine.
- **Use Technology:** Share your location with a trusted friend or family member when going out. Use safety **apps that quickly alert emergency contacts if you feel unsafe.**
- **Enable GPS tracking** on your phone when heading out alone, especially in new locations.

Self-Defense Items:

- **Consider carrying items like pepper or bug spray, a whistle, or a personal alarm**. Make sure you know how to use these items **effectively.**
- **Place items in cars and rooms where they are easily accessible**.
- **I carry a knuckle cracker in my vehicle** beside my coffee holder. Also, a large police flashlight with a buried knife. Either when used, it will break a window or a hand.
- **Another favorite is Wasp Spray**, which shoots 50 feet. Some of my schoolteachers keep these in their desk drawers.

Implementing these tips can significantly enhance personal safety and provide a sense of peace of mind. Always remember to trust your instincts and take proactive measures to protect yourself.

By understanding the historical context and learning from the past, we empower ourselves with the knowledge and skills to navigate today's dangerous world with confidence and safety.

Whether you are a woman seeking to enhance your safety, a parent guiding a teenager, or an educator or advocate working to support women's rights, this book provides valuable insights and practical solutions.

References - Books and Websites

1. Challenges Faced by Women (1970s–1990s)

- **Domestic Violence & Legal Protections**
  – NCADV, "Domestic Violence." NCADV. Retrieved from NCADV
  – Violence Against Women Act (VAWA) of 1994. U.S. Congress. Available at Congress.gov

- **Business Travel**
  – Fels, A. (2004). *Necessary Dreams: Ambition in Women's Changing Lives*. Harvard University Press.
  – Babin, B. J. & Boles, J. S. (1996). "Co-worker involvement & supervisor support…" *Journal of Retailing*.

- **Rural vs. Urban Violence**
  – Logan, T. K., Walker, R. & Hoyt, W. (2012). "The Rural Context…" *Trauma, Violence, & Abuse*, 13(3), 201–221.
  – Peek-Asa, C. et al. (2011). "Rural disparity in domestic violence…" *Journal of Women's Health*, 20(11), 1743–1749.

- **Intersection of Race & IPV**
  – CDC, NISVS 2010–12 State Report. Available at CDC NISVS
  – Richie, B. E. (2012). *Arrested Justice: Black Women, Violence, and America's Prison Nation*. NYU Press.

- **Religious-Institution Abuse**
  – Browne, A. & Finkelhor, D. (1986). "Impact of Child Sexual Abuse..." *Psychological Bulletin*, 99(1), 66–77.
  – Finkelhor, D. & Williams, L. M. (1988). *License to Rape: Sexual Abuse of Wives*. Free Press.

- **Violence in Sports**
  – USA Gymnastics Abuse Scandal: public reports & court documents.
  – Kerr, G., Willson, E. & Stirling, A. (2020). "The Safe Sport Movement..." *International Review for the Sociology of Sport*, 55(5), 555–574.

2. Books on Fear & Self-Defense

- Jeffers, S. L., *Feel the Fear and Do It Anyway*

- de Becker, G., *The Gift of Fear*

- Bishop, G. J., *Unfuk Yourself**

- Kardian, S., *The New Superpower for Women*

- Larkin, T., *When Violence Is the Answer*

3. Self-Defense Law & Support Resources

- **Law Overviews**
  – Cornell LII, Self-Defense
  – NCSL, Stand Your Ground & Castle Doctrine

- **Domestic Violence & VAWA**
  – ABA Commission on Domestic & Sexual Violence: americanbar.org
  – National Domestic Violence Hotline: thehotline.org
  – DOJ, Office on Violence Against Women: justice.gov/ovw
  – White House Fact Sheet on VAWA Reauthorization: whitehouse.gov

- **General Legal Aid**
  – Legal Aid Society: legalaid.org
  – FindLaw, Self-Defense Overview

4. Workplace & School Violence Prevention

- **Federal Laws & Guidelines**
  – OSHA, Violence Prevention for Healthcare & Social Service Workers
  – EEOC, Title VII Guidance
  – ADA Regulations & Guidance: ada.gov

- **State Laws**
  – Cal/OSHA Healthcare Violence Prevention Law
  – NY Workplace Violence Prevention Act

- **Sector-Specific Data & Programs**
  – NCES, School Safety Reports
  – APA, Violence in Schools & Healthcare
  – ANA, Nursing Workplace Violence Resources
  – NEA, School Safety Resources
  – Kaiser Permanente Violence Prevention Strategies
  – NYC DOE Anti-Violence Initiative
  – UTMB BERT Program Overview

5. Cyberbullying Resources

- StopBullying.gov

- PACER National Bullying Prevention Center

- Cyberbullying Research Center

- Common Sense Media

- Child Mind Institute

- Netsmartz (NCMEC)

- The Trevor Project

- Stomp Out Bullying

6. Misc. Online Safety & Risk Resources

- https://www.domesticviolenceinfo.ca/resources

- https://just2seconds.org/

- https://advisorsmith.com/data/most-dangerous-jobs/

- https://www.insurdinary.ca/what-are-the-most-dangerous-jobs-in-canada/

- https://info.apartmentguardian.com/blog/is-working-in-real-estate-dangerous-heres-what-the-statistics-say

- https://www.paloaltoonline.com/real-estate/2023/09/20/showing-property-can-be-a-dangerous-job/

- https://propertyonion.com/education/trend-of-violence-against-women-real-estate-agents/

- RAINN: rainn.org

- https://www.yahoo.com/lifestyle/man-bear-hypothetical-sparks-conversation-021728031.html
- https://www.elephantjournal.com/2024/05/man-vs-bear-why-some-women-are-choosing-the-bear-michelle-schafer/
- https://www.goodreads.com/work/quotes/1212277-the-gift-of-fear

Biography

Teacher, Analyst, Researcher, Author

Joanne Morin Correia

With a 2nd-degree Black Belt, served as an instructor at the National Academy of Self-Defense Education, teaching RAD Systems training in Basic (for Women, Men, and Kids) and advanced courses in Weapons and Keychain Defense.

At R+H Taekwondo (NH) and in Florida, conducted medical safety programs in First Aid and AED/CPR for children, women, and seniors.

Joanne was certified by Zumba Fitness, RAD Systems, and the American Red Cross and is a proud member of the Black Belt Club in Moo Duk Kwan, Taekwondo.

Quotes from our past students

- "My friends and I were so impressed and grateful for all we learned in our weekend class!" - Family Doctor

- "I recommend your self-defense course to women of all ages. I found your teaching style to be very easy to follow. You adjusted to meet the needs of the various ages in the class." - Registered Nurse

- "Joanne and her son Jonathan provided us with priceless information and skills that could one day save our lives!" - Fitness Instructor

- "I know a huge part of my trip's success was due to the training I received from you!" - AIDS Clinic Volunteer, South Africa.

**See our other books and workshops at
www.commonsensesafetyclasses.com**

Common Sense Safety for Women

Using Common Sense for Self-Defense

© 2025 Common Sense Safety Classes

www.ingramcontent.com/pod-product-compliance
Lightning Source LLC
Chambersburg PA
CBHW060042150626
46556CB00018BA/2596